Level **1**

4th Edition

Listening & Notetaking Skills

Without Audioscripts

D1314875

Patricia A. Dunkel & Phyllis L. Lim

With

Christine Salica Seal

NATIONAL GEOGRAPHIC LEARNING |  HEINLE CENGAGE Learning

Australia • Brazil • Japan • Korea • Mexico • Singapore • Spain • United Kingdom • United States

Listening and Notetaking Skills 1,
Fourth Edition
Without Audioscripts
Patricia A. Dunkel and Phyllis L. Lim

Publisher: Sherrise Roehr

Executive Editor: Laura Le Dréan

Director of Global Marketing: Ian Martin

International Marketing Manager: Caitlin Thomas

Product Manager: Emily Stewart

Director, Content and Media Production:
Michael Burggren

Content Project Manager: Andrea Bobotas

Print Buyer: Mary Beth Hennebury

Cover Designers: Christopher Roy and
Michael Rosenquest

Cover Image: Frans Lanting/National Geographic
Stock

Compositor: Page Designs International

Copyright © 2015, 2006, 1994 National Geographic Learning, a part of
Cengage Learning

ALL RIGHTS RESERVED. No part of this work covered by the copyright herein may
be reproduced, transmitted, stored, or used in any form or by any means graphic,
electronic, or mechanical, including but not limited to photocopying, recording,
scanning, digitizing, taping, Web distribution, information networks, or information
storage and retrieval systems, except as permitted under Section 107 or 108 of the
1976 United States Copyright Act, or applicable copyright law of another jurisdiction,
without the prior written permission of the publisher.

For product information and technology assistance, contact us at
Cengage Learning Customer & Sales Support,
1-800-354-9706

For permission to use material from this text or product,
submit all requests online at **www.cengage.com/permissions**.
Further permissions questions can be e-mailed to
permissionrequest@cengage.com.

Student Book ISBN: 978-1-305-49342-1

National Geographic Learning
20 Channel Center Street
Boston, MA 02210
USA

Cengage Learning is a leading provider of customized learning solutions with
office locations around the globe, including Singapore, the United Kingdom,
Australia, Mexico, Brazil and Japan.

Cengage Learning products are represented in Canada by Nelson Education, Ltd.

Visit National Geographic Learning online at **ngl.cengage.com.**

Visit our corporate website at **www.cengage.com.**

Printed in the United States of America
Print Number: 01   Print Year: 2014

CONTENTS

SCOPE AND SEQUENCE

	Unit		Chapter	

Notetaking Preparation	Expansion	Unit Video
• Notetaking Basics: Abbreviations and Symbols	**Task 1:** Famous Historical Figures **Task 2:** The History of the Bicycle	 **Surviving an Avalanche**
• Using Symbols in Notes	**Task 1:** What Happened First? **Task 2:** Famous Volcanoes of the World	
• Time Lines	**Task 1:** The Evolution of the Computer **Task 2:** Landmarks in Technology	
• Steps in a Process	**Task 1:** Taking a Pulse **Task 2:** Yoga Poses	 **Tristan da Cunha Oil Spill**
• Abbreviating Frequently Repeated Words	**Task 1:** Stages in Language Development **Task 2:** Writing an E-mail	
• Listening for New Sections of a Lecture	**Task 1:** Steps in Doing Research **Task 2:** A Simple Experiment	
• Recording Definitions	**Task 1:** Listening for Definitions **Task 2:** Natural Disasters	 **People, Plants, and Pollinators**
• Listening for Examples	**Task 1:** Homonyms and Homophones **Task 2:** Classifying Parts of Speech	
• Listening for Classifying Language	**Task 1:** Classifying Animals **Task 2:** What's That Animal?	
• Making a Comparison Chart	**Task 1:** The Hippo and the Rhino **Task 2:** Two Brothers	 **Free Soloing with Alex Honnold**
• Listening to the Lecture Overview	**Task 1:** Two First Ladies **Task 2:** Two Vice Presidents	
• Making Your Notes Complete	**Task 1:** The Hindenburg Disaster **Task 2:** Easily Confused Words	
• Using Arrows for Cause and Effect	**Task 1:** What's the Reason? **Task 2:** You Write the Ending	 **The Surma People**
• When Not to Take Notes	**Task 1:** The Revolutionary War **Task 2:** Guessing Causes	
• Listening for a Review of the Lecture	**Task 1:** Endangered Species **Task 2:** Types of Pollution	

UNIT WALKTHROUGH

New to This Edition

- Authentic **National Geographic videos** provide a meaningful context for discussion and application of essential listening, notetaking, and vocabulary skills.

- New and updated **academic lectures** offer compelling, cross-curricular content that simulate authentic scenarios for maximum academic readiness.

- Every unit introduces a focused aspect of **notetaking** and provides varied opportunities for practice and application of the skill.

UNIT

4

Comparison and Contrast

Describing Similarities and Differences

A Great Dane and a little Chihuahua

Learners prepare for notetaking in the academic classroom through focused instruction and practice on organizational modes such as Chronology, Process, and Cause and Effect.

Before Listening activities prepare students for success by activating background knowledge and providing the language and skills necessary for comprehension.

CHAPTER

10

Asian and African Elephants

Similarities and Differences

TOPIC PREVIEW

Answer the following questions with a partner or your classmates.

1. Discuss the animals you see in the photo on this page. What do you know about these animals?

2. Have you ever seen a real elephant? Describe where and when you saw it. What impressed you most about the animal?

3. Talk about the similarities and differences between elephants (the largest animals that live on land) and whales (the largest animals that live in water).

A young elephant in Kaziranga National Park, India

BEFORE LISTENING

VOCABULARY PREVIEW

🔊 **A** Listen to the following sentences that contain information from the lecture. As you listen, write the word from the box that completes the sentence.

| enormous | fascinating | mammals | tamer | temperament |
| trained | trunk | tusks | wilder | |

1. Today's topic is the largest land _____ on earth—elephants.

2. Elephants are _____ animals.

3. An elephant uses its _____ to put grasses, leaves, and water into its mouth.

4. Elephants can be _____ to do heavy work.

5. The Asian elephant sometimes does not have any _____ at all.

6. A big difference between the two types of elephants is their _____

7. The Asian elephant is _____ than the African elephant.

8. The African elephant is much _____ than the Asian elephant.

9. There certainly are differences between the African and the Asian elephants, but they are both _____ animals.

B Match the words to their definitions.

_____ 1. mammal   a. the long nose of an elephant

_____ 2. enormous   b. to teach to do something

_____ 3. fascinating   c. easy for people to control and teach

_____ 4. tame   d. one of the two long teeth that an elephant has

_____ 5. temperament   e. very difficult for people to control

_____ 6. train   f. of very great or large size; huge

_____ 7. trunk   g. very interesting

_____ 8. tusk   h. nature; outlook; personality

_____ 9. wild   i. an animal that feeds its own milk to its babies

PREDICTIONS

Think about the questions in the Topic Preview on page 74 and the sentences you heard in the Vocabulary Preview. Write three questions that you think will be answered in the lecture. Share your questions with your classmates.

The *Notetaking Preparation* section presents a variety of effective notetaking techniques. Using content from the unit, students practice these techniques in authentic academic situations.

Notetaking Skills

Throughout the *Listening & Notetaking Skills* series, learners develop a wide variety of notetaking strategies necessary for academic success. Learners are taught the essential principles of notetaking and encouraged to personalize the strategies for maximum results.

NOTETAKING PREPARATION

Making a Comparison Chart

As soon as a lecturer indicates that he or she is going to compare or contrast two things, a good notetaker will make a chart with two columns and put the name of the two things that are going to be compared at the top of the columns.

X	Y

Listen for statements such as

There are two types of
Today I am going to be talking about X and Y
Today's lecture will compare and contrast X and Y

A well-planned lecture will compare each point in an organized way so that you can list each of the points opposite each other in the chart. When something is the same on both sides of the chart, you can save time by just putting a check (✓) in the second column.

🔊 **A** Listen to this short talk about two types of camels. As you listen, make a chart below and write in some details about each kind of camel.

Discourse Cues for Comparison and Contrast Listen for language that indicates that the lecturer is making a comparison. Key words and phrases to listen for are:

Both X and Y . . .
One/another similarity is that X and Y . . .
X and Y are alike in that . . .

🔊 **B** Listen to part of the lecture. As you listen, count the number of times that the lecturer uses the word *both*. Circle your answer below.

a. 2   b. 3   c. 4   d. 5

LISTENING

🔊 **FIRST LISTENING**

Listen to the lecture on elephants. As you listen, put the following parts of the lecture in the order that you hear them. Number them 1 to 5.

_____ The continents elephants come from

_____ Elephants' temperaments

_____ Elephants' trunks

_____ Elephants' size

_____ Elephants' intelligence

🔊 **SECOND LISTENING**

Listen to information from the lecture. The speaker will talk slowly and carefully. You don't have to do anything as you listen. Just relax and listen.

THIRD LISTENING

Listen to the lecture in two parts. Follow the directions for each part. When you have finished, review your notes. Later, you will use them to summarize the lecture with a partner.

🔊 **Part 1**

You will hear the first part of the lecture again. Listen and complete the notes by adding the abbreviations and symbols from the box.

| ✓ | e.g. | gals | + | Afr. |

Asian E	E
has trunk	✓
eats leaves + grass	
picks up obj _____ trees	
drinks 50 _____ H₂O per day	
intellgnt	✓
heavy work	
do tricks _____ entertain	

🔊 **Part 2**

As you listen to the second part of the lecture, take your own notes on a separate piece of paper.

Listening sections introduce the academic lecture. Learners listen to the lecture three times, focusing on a different listening and notetaking skill with each repetition.

After Listening sections provide learners with opportunities to discuss the lecture through pair and group activities.

ACCURACY CHECK

A You will hear four questions about the lecture. Listen to each question and write the letter of the best answer.

_____ 1. a. ear
b. trunk
c. tooth
d. tusk

_____ 2. a. African elephants
b. Asian elephants
c. both Asian and African
d. neither African nor Asian

_____ 3. a. 7,000 to 12,000 lbs.
b. 8,000 to 10,000 lbs.
c. 12,000 to 14,000 lbs.
d. 18,000 to 20,000 lbs.

_____ 4. a. larger and lighter
b. heavier and larger
c. lighter and smaller
d. smaller and heavier

B You will hear five statements about the lecture. Listen to each statement and decide if you heard the information in the lecture. Write *Y* for *yes* or *N* for *no*.

1. _____   2. _____   3. _____   4. _____   5. _____

The *Oral Summary* asks learners to use their notes to reconstruct the content of the lecture.

ORAL SUMMARY

Use your notes to create an oral summary of the lecture with your partner. As you work together, add details to your notes that your partner included but you had missed.

Through guided prompts, *Discussion* activities provide opportunities for learners to hone communicative and critical thinking skills.

DISCUSSION

Discuss the following questions with a classmate or in a small group.

1. Some people say the one animal that doesn't belong in a zoo is the elephant. Do you agree? Why? Do you think there are animals other than elephants that don't belong in zoos or circuses?

2. Compare two domestic animals (dog, cat, horse, etc.) and two wild animals (giraffe, bear, wolf, etc.). How are the two domestic animals similar and different? How are the two wild animals similar and different?

3. Some Asian elephants are working animals that are trained to do work such as lifting tree trunks for people. What animals do work in your country? What work do they do?

4. How are the kinds of pets sold in pet stores and those given away by animal rescue organizations such as the ASPCA similar or different?

The *Expansion* section in each chapter provides opportunities for learners to broaden their knowledge of the featured rhetorical mode through a variety of listening and critical thinking activities.

TASK 1 The Hippo and the Rhino

A Listen to the talk about the similarities and differences between the hippopotamus—the hippo—and the rhinoceros—the rhino. As you listen, complete the Venn diagram with the information below.

herbivores	loners
have horns	very big and heavy
endangered	eat at night	social animals	can be found in Asia
good swimmers	can be found in Africa

Hippos   Rhinos

B Compare your answers with a partner and make sentences that compare and contrast the two animals.

TASK 2 Two Brothers

A Listen for similarities and differences between two brothers, Charlie and David. As you listen, put a check (✓) in the correct box under each picture.

Charlie		David
☐	is married	☐
☐	has two children	☐
☐	has a girl and a boy	☐
☐	works in an office	☐
☐	works as a firefighter	☐
☐	likes jazz music	☐
☐	likes to play golf	☐
☐	is wealthy	☐

B Compare your answers with a partner.

Unit Video

Each unit ends with an authentic **National Geographic** video that is related to the unit theme. Most of the videos are in a lecture format, giving students a further opportunity to practice notetaking skills.

UNIT 4
VIDEO

Free Soloing with Alex Honnold

B Work with a partner and discuss answers to the following questions.

1. Is there anything that is **well within your ability** to do but not easy for other people that you know?
2. Does your life **revolve around** a particular person, place, or activity?
3. In what areas can some people be **unbelievably gifted**?
4. What special **gear** do you need to do an activity that you enjoy doing?
5. Describe a time when you decided to stop doing something and to **switch** and do something different.
6. At what age do you think you were **at the top of your game**?
7. What experiences have you had that you would describe as "**awesome**" or "**memorable moments**"?

BEFORE VIEWING

TOPIC PREVIEW

Work with a partner to make a list or draw pictures in the box below. Draw or list the different pieces of equipment mountain climbers use to keep them safe when they climb.

VOCABULARY PREVIEW

A Read the definitions of these key words and phrases that you will hear during the video.

gear special equipment used to do a particular activity or sport
at the top of [this] game at the very highest level of ability
unbelievably gifted with an amazing, incredible natural talent
revolves around turns in a circle about a central point that is the focus
memorable moments times that are so enjoyable or important in your life that you expect you will always remember them
switched changed
well within his ability something that he could easily do
awesome amazing, extraordinary, fantastic, wonderful

VIEWING

📺 FIRST VIEWING

Watch the video, and then compare your first impressions with a partner. Talk about what you remember, what surprised you, and what interested you.

📺 SECOND VIEWING

Watch the video again. Listen for the missing words and write them in the blanks.

1. Free soloing has to be the ultimate in free _____.
2. The reason it's probably the ultimate is because one _____ move, you fall, you die.
3. Yeah, I would say that Yosemite probably is the _____ of my climbing.
4. For most people on this planet who are serious climbers, doing Half Dome in a day or two is considered _____. Alex did it in three hours, without a _____.
5. I've sort of embraced the whole _____, you know, embraced the unpleasant parts, too.

Half Dome, Yosemite National Park

Listening and Notetaking Skills Series Components

The Audio CDs provide all the lectures and listening activities contained in the Student Book.

The Video DVD contains five authentic **National Geographic** videos relating to the units in the book.

Chronology
Talking about When Things Happen

Photographs of an eclipse taken at five-minute intervals

Napoleon

From Schoolboy to Emperor

TOPIC PREVIEW

Answer the following questions with a partner or your classmates.

1. Who was Napoleon Bonaparte? What is he famous for?

2. When do you think Napoleon was born?

3. How are Alexander the Great, Julius Caesar, and George Washington like Napoleon? Do you know any dates of the important events in these people's lives?

Napoleon Bonaparte

VOCABULARY PREVIEW

CD 1, TR 1

A Listen to the following sentences that contain information from the lecture. As you listen, write the word from the box that completes the sentence.

campaign	controlled	deserted	emperor
excelled	fame	figures	victories

1. One of the most important historical _____ in European history was Napoleon Bonaparte.

2. Napoleon _____ in mathematics and military science.

3. In 1785, Napoleon began the military career that brought him _____, power, riches, and, finally, defeat.

4. Napoleon won many _____ on the battlefield.

5. Napoleon became the first _____ of France.

6. At one time, Napoleon _____ most of Europe.

7. In his military _____ against Russia, Napoleon lost most of his army.

8. The great French conqueror died alone, _____ by his family and friends.

B Match the words to their definitions.

_____ 1. desert   a. a planned series of actions against an enemy

_____ 2. fame   b. to leave all alone

_____ 3. control   c. the recognition of many people for something you did

_____ 4. victory

_____ 5. emperor   d. a person, usually someone important in a particular way

_____ 6. campaign   e. success in winning a competition or war

_____ 7. figure   f. to have power or authority over something

_____ 8. excel   g. to do extremely well

     h. the ruler of a group of countries

PREDICTIONS

Think about the questions in the Topic Preview on page 2 and the sentences you heard in the Vocabulary Preview. Write three questions that you think will be answered in the lecture. Share your questions with your classmates.

NOTETAKING PREPARATION

Notetaking Basics: Abbreviations and Symbols

When you listen to a lecture and take notes, you have to write down a lot of information very quickly. Don't try to write every word. Use symbols and abbreviations as much as possible.

- Abbreviate names, places, and titles by using the first letter or the first several letters. You can use a period, but when taking notes, this isn't always necessary.

  R. (Rita)   S. (Steve)   US (United States)
  S.A. (South America)   Prof (Professor)   Gen (General)
  Pres (President)   dir. (director)

- Abbreviate important words in a lecture by shortening them.

  exc (excelled)   milit sch (military school)
  fath (father)   bril (brilliant)

- Use symbols to indicate relationships between things.

  & (and)   = (equals, is, has)
  ≠ (not, not the same as)   @ (at)

CD 1, TR 2

A Listen to information from the lecture. Match the notes below to the information you hear. Write the number of the sentence in the blank.

_____ N. = exc math & milit sc

_____ @ 16 Fr. arm

_____ N. ≠ gd stud

_____ att Rus. & defeated

_____ N. died 1821 @ 51

Discourse Cues for Chronology In a lecture with historical information, listen for dates. In English, when a year is given, the speaker will first give the number for the century, for example, *eighteen*; and then the number within the century, for example, *twenty-three*. So 1823 is said, *eighteen twenty-three*. When the year is in the first decade of the century, however, the speaker will say, *O five, O six, O seven,* and so on. So 1902 is said, *nineteen O two.*

CD 1, TR 2

B Listen to four dates. As you listen, write the dates as numbers in the spaces below.

1. _____   3. _____

2. _____   4. _____

🔊 FIRST LISTENING
CD 1, TR 3

Listen to the lecture about Napoleon. As you listen, put the following parts of the lecture in the order that you hear them. Number them 1 to 5.

_____ Napoleon is all alone.

_____ Napoleon controls most of Europe.

_____ Napoleon lives on Corsica.

_____ Napoleon becomes Emperor of France.

_____ Napoleon attacks Russia.

🔊 SECOND LISTENING
CD 1, TR 4

Listen to information from the lecture. The speaker will talk slowly and carefully. You don't have to do anything as you listen. Just relax and listen.

THIRD LISTENING

Listen to the lecture in two parts. Follow the directions for each part. When you have finished, review your notes. Later, you will use them to summarize the lecture with a partner.

🔊 CD 1, TR 5

Part 1

You will hear the first part of the lecture again. Listen and complete the notes by adding the abbreviations and symbols from the box.

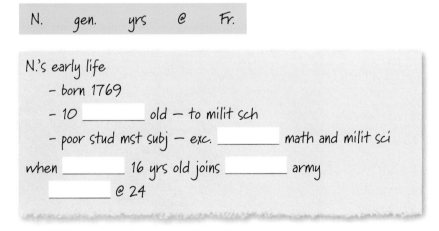

| N. | gen. | yrs | @ | Fr. |

N.'s early life
- born 1769
- 10 _____ old – to milit sch
- poor stud mst subj – exc. _____ math and milit sci
when _____ 16 yrs old joins _____ army
_____ @ 24

🔊 CD 1, TR 5

Part 2

As you listen to the second part of the lecture, take your own notes on a separate piece of paper.

ACCURACY CHECK

CD 1, TR 6

You will hear questions and statements about the lecture. For 1–4, listen to the question and write the letter of the best answer. For 5–8, listen to the statement and write *T* for *true* or *F* for *false*.

_____ 1. a. in 1821
      b. in France
      c. in 1769
      d. in Corsica

_____ 3. a. power
      b. wealth
      c. defeat
      d. all of the above

_____ 2. a. outstanding
      b. excellent
      c. good
      d. poor

_____ 4. a. when he was 51 years old
      b. in 1804
      c. after he attacked Russia
      d. just before he defeated England

5. _____   6. _____   7. _____   8. _____

ORAL SUMMARY

Use your notes to create an oral summary of the lecture with your partner. As you work together, add details to your notes that your partner included but you had missed.

DISCUSSION

Discuss the following statements with a classmate or in a small group.

1. Napoleon was a great man.

2. It would be impossible today for a person to have a career like Napoleon's.

3. Ten-year-old children are too young to be sent to a military school.

4. Every young man and woman should be required to do at least two years of military service for his or her country.

TASK 1 Famous Historical Figures

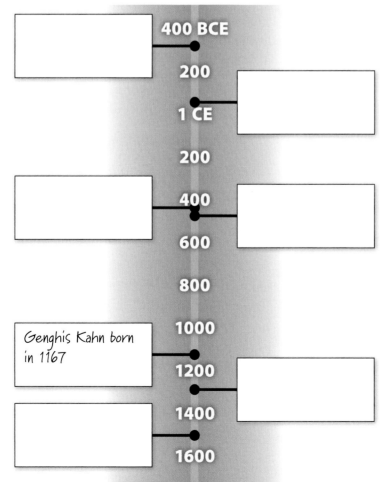

🔊
CD 1, TR 7

A Listen to six short biographies of famous figures in history. As you listen, fill in the missing information in the sentences below. The first one is done for you.

1. I lived in Central _____Asia_____. I ruled a large empire. I am Genghis Kahn, born in _____1167_____.

2. I am _____ the Great. I became ruler of my people in _____ BCE.

3. In _____ I traveled to China. I am from _____. My name is Marco Polo.

4. I am Suleiman the Magnificent. I ruled the _____ Empire from the year _____.

5. I am from _____. I was a great queen who died at age 39 in _____ BCE.

6. My name brings fear to many. I was born around the year _____. In _____ I conquered Gaul. I am _____ the Hun.

B Work with a partner and complete the time line below. Use information from the sentences in **A** above. The first one is done for you.

400 BCE

200

1 CE

200

400

600

800

1000

Genghis Kahn born in 1167

1200

1400

1600

1800

Statue of Genghis Kahn

TASK 2 The History of the Bicycle

CD 1, TR 8

A **Listen to a short history of the bicycle. As you listen and read, write the missing information in the blank spaces. The first one is done for you.**

History of the Bicycle

The earliest "bicycle" appeared in France in the _____1790s_____ . It was a little
wooden horse with a front wheel that could not be turned right or left. This little horse did
not have any pedals, and the only way it could be moved was by the rider pushing against
the ground with his or her feet.

In _____ , the German baron Karl von Drais made a front wheel that
could turn. Now the rider could direct the wooden horse right or left. The rider still needed
to push it with his or her feet on the ground.

The next development occurred in _____ , when a Scottish blacksmith,
Kirkpatrick MacMillan, designed the first bicyclelike machine with pedals. MacMillan rode
his machine the 70 miles from his home to Glasgow, Scotland, in only _____ .

In _____ Pierre Lallement applied for and received a U.S. patent for a
machine that he called the "bisicle." Some people called it a "boneshaker" because it had
steel wheels. _____ later, in 1869, rubber tires were introduced
and the bicycle got more comfortable. Around the same time, the
front wheels began to get larger and the back wheels got smaller.

The first "highwheeler" was introduced in 1872. During the
_____ , bicycles enjoyed a sudden growth in
popularity. The highwheelers were very popular, especially
among young men. They could go very fast, but they weren't
very safe. A rider sitting high up on the bicycle and traveling
very fast could easily fall off if the bicycle hit even a small
bump in the road.

Fortunately, the "safety bicycle" was invented in
_____ . The safety bicycle had equal-sized wheels, a
chain, and a gear-driven rear wheel. The rider was now sitting further back on the bicycle
and in less danger. More improvements followed. Pneumatic tires—that is, tires with air in
them—were invented in _____ . The last major innovation, the derailleur gear,
arrived _____ after that, in 1899.

Beginning in the _____ , bicycles became lighter, and changes in design
and materials allowed bicycles to go faster. No doubt there will be more improvements in
design and materials in the future.

B **Check your answers with a partner.**

Pompeii

Destroyed, Forgotten, and Found

TOPIC PREVIEW

Answer the following questions with a partner or your classmates.

1. Where is the city of Pompeii? What natural disaster happened there about 2,000 years ago?

2. Have you or someone you know ever experienced a natural disaster? What happened?

3. Name one or two cities somewhere in the world that are in danger if a nearby volcano erupts or explodes. What would happen to those cities?

The ruins of Pompeii with Mount Vesuvius in background

VOCABULARY PREVIEW

CD 1, TR 9

A Listen to the following sentences that contain information from the lecture. As you listen, write the word from the box that completes the sentence.

archaeologists	ancient	ash	CE
eruption	metropolitan	ruins	volcanic

1. Many rich people who live in large _____ areas leave the city in the summer and go to the mountains or to the seashore.

2. In the summer of the year 79 _____, a young Roman boy was visiting his uncle at Pompeii.

3. Pliny saw the _____ of the volcano called Mount Vesuvius.

4. Rock and _____ flew through the air.

5. When the eruption was over, Pompeii was buried under 20 feet of _____ rock and ash.

6. In 1748, an Italian farmer digging on his farm uncovered part of a wall of the _____ city of Pompeii.

7. Soon, _____ began to dig in the area.

8. Today, tourists come from all over the world to see the _____ of the famous city of Pompeii.

B Match the words to their definitions.

_____ 1. archeologist

_____ 2. ash

_____ 3. volcanic

_____ 4. ancient

_____ 5. eruption

_____ 6. metropolitan

_____ 7. ruins

_____ 8. CE

a. the time when a volcano explodes and sends hot rock and dust into the air

b. very old or from many years earlier

c. a scientist who studies things left by people who lived long ago

d. the Common Era

e. the remains of destroyed buildings or cities

f. from a volcano

g. a soft, gray powder that is left when something burns

h. of or connected to a large city

PREDICTIONS

Think about the questions in the Topic Preview on page 9 and the sentences you heard in the Vocabulary Preview. Write three questions that you think will be answered in the lecture. Share your questions with your classmates.

NOTETAKING PREPARATION

Using Symbols in Notes

As you learned in Chapter 1, you can use symbols to get information down quickly. Several of these symbols come from mathematics.

< less than

> more than

~ about, approximately

→ leads to, then, next, become, go to

↓ not so many, get less, down

↑ many, increase, up

+ and, also, more than

∴ therefore, as a result

number

K thousand

🔊
CD 1, TR 10

A **Listen to the sentences that contain information from the lecture. As you listen, complete each of the following notes with one of the symbols from the box above.**

1. boy look _____ in sky

2. boy _____ fam Rom. historian

3. no time to escape _____ buried alive

4. _____ 2000 ppl died

5. P. forgotten _____ 1700 yrs

Discourse Cues for Chronology Listen carefully for words and phrases that tell you when something happened and the order in which something happened. Such words and phrases are particularly important when someone is telling a story.

in [year]	today / one day	for [length of time]
in the winter of [year]	a few years later	as / after / before
[length of time] ago	after [number] years	then / next / later

🔊
CD 1, TR 10

B **Listen to information from the lecture and write down the chronological discourse cues you hear.**

1. _____

2. _____

3. _____

4. _____

5. _____

🔊 FIRST LISTENING
CD 1, TR 11

Listen to the lecture on Pompeii. As you listen, put the following parts of the lecture in the order that you hear them. Number them 1 to 5.

_____ Mount Vesuvius erupted.

_____ Tourists visit the ruins of Pompeii.

_____ Pliny the Younger went to visit Pompeii.

_____ Eighteen thousand people escaped from Pompeii.

_____ Pompeii was completely buried.

🔊 SECOND LISTENING
CD 1, TR 12

Listen to information from the lecture. The speaker will talk slowly and carefully. You don't have to do anything as you listen. Just relax and listen.

THIRD LISTENING

Listen to the lecture in two parts. Follow the directions for each part. When you have finished, review your notes. Later, you will use them to summarize the lecture with a partner.

🔊
CD 1, TR 13

Part 1

You will hear the first part of the lecture again. Listen and complete the notes by adding the abbreviations and symbols from the box.

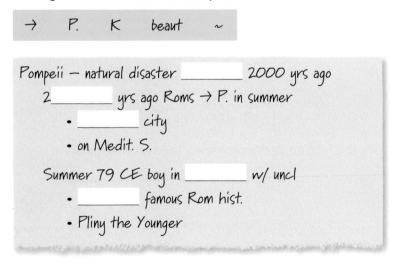

🔊
CD 1, TR 13

Part 2

As you listen to the second part of the lecture, take your own notes on a separate piece of paper.

ACCURACY CHECK

CD 1, TR 14

You will hear questions and statements about the lecture. For 1–4, listen to the question and write the letter of the best answer. For 5–8, listen to the statement and write T for *true* or F for *false*.

_____ 1. a. for holidays
   b. in the summer
   c. in the fall
   d. for vacation

_____ 2. a. 2000 CE
   b. 1748 CE
   c. 79 CE
   d. 1800 CE

_____ 3. a. a volcano
   b. a dark cloud
   c. a mountain
   d. an eruption

_____ 4. a. 79 CE
   b. 2,000 years ago
   c. 1748
   d. 2000 CE

5. _____   6. _____   7. _____   8. _____

ORAL SUMMARY

Use your notes to create an oral summary of the lecture with your partner. As you work together, add details to your notes that your partner included but you had missed.

DISCUSSION

Discuss the following questions with a classmate or in a small group.

1. Why do you think the lecturer explained that Pliny the Younger became a famous historian?

2. If you had lived in Pompeii in 79 CE, what would you have done when the volcano began to erupt?

3. Name some disaster movies that you are familiar with. Why do you think so many people enjoy watching disaster movies?

4. The eruption of Vesuvius was a *natural* disaster that could not be prevented. But other disasters can be prevented, for example, an explosion at a nuclear power plant. What do you think is the most dangerous situation today that could cause a disaster? What do you think people can do to change the situation?

TASK 1 What Happened First?

CD 1, TR 15

A Listen to two sentences. For each pair of sentences, take notes as your listen.

1.

2.

3.

4.

5.

6.

CD 1, TR 15

B Listen to the two sentences again. Circle *before* if the event in the first sentence happened before the event in the second sentence. Circle *after* if it happened after.

1. The event in Sentence 1 happened **before / after** the event in Sentence 2.

2. The event in Sentence 1 happened **before / after** the event in Sentence 2.

3. The event in Sentence 1 happened **before / after** the event in Sentence 2.

4. The event in Sentence 1 happened **before / after** the event in Sentence 2.

5. The event in Sentence 1 happened **before / after** the event in Sentence 2.

6. The event in Sentence 1 happened **before / after** the event in Sentence 2.

TASK 2 Famous Volcanoes of the World

A Listen to the short lecture. As you listen, fill in the missing information about the famous volcanoes in the chart below.

CD 1, TR 16

Famous Volcanoes of the World			
Name	**Location**	**Date of Eruption**	**Approximate Number of People Who Died**
Vesuvius	Italy	79	2,000
Cotopaxi	Ecuador	1877	
Krakatoa	Indonesia		36,000
Mont Pelée	Martinique	1902	
Mount St. Helens	Washington State (U.S.A.)	1980	
Mount Tambora	Indonesia		

B Check your answers with a partner.

Eruption of Mount Tungurahua in Ecuador

Steve Jobs

A Man with a Vision

TOPIC PREVIEW

Answer the following questions with a partner or your classmates.

1. What electronic tools—a computer, a cell phone, a tablet, etc.—do you use on a daily basis? Which is the one you could not do without? Why?

2. Describe an electronic device you dream of having 25 years from now. Why do you think this type of device would be helpful both to you and others?

3. Who are two people who you think are as famous as Steve Jobs? Explain why.

Steve Jobs

VOCABULARY PREVIEW

CD 1, TR 17

A Listen to the following sentences that contain information from the lecture. As you listen, write the word from the box that completes the sentence.

animated	device	equipment	founded
mass	profitable	released	strategy

1. Jobs' friend Stephen Wozniak liked to design and build his own electronic

   _____ .

2. Jobs and Wozniak _____ the Apple Computer company.

3. The Apple II became the world's first _____-produced personal computer.

4. The movie *Toy Story* was the first full-length, computer-generated,

   _____ film.

5. Pixar became a very, very _____ company.

6. In 2001 Jobs introduced Apple's "digital-hub" _____ .

7. The iPhone was like having a computer, a camera, and a phone all in one

   _____ .

8. Three years later, Jobs _____ the iPad onto the market.

B Match the words to their definitions.

_____ 1. equipment   a. in large numbers

_____ 2. found   b. a method or plan for doing something

_____ 3. mass   c. made by filming many slightly different pictures so they appear to move

_____ 4. animated

_____ 5. profitable   d. makes a lot of money for you or your company

_____ 6. strategy   e. to start a business

_____ 7. device   f. to make a product available for sale

_____ 8. release   g. tools or other items used for a particular purpose

     h. a machine used for a special purpose

PREDICTIONS

Think about the questions in the Topic Preview on page 16 and the sentences you heard in the Vocabulary Preview. Write three questions that you think will be answered in the lecture. Share your questions with your classmates.

NOTETAKING PREPARATION

Time Lines

When you are taking notes about a person's life, write the dates and years that you hear underneath one another in the left margin of your notes. Then after the lecture, you can easily turn your notes into a time line that will help you organize the events in that person's life.

1955	Bill Gates b. in Seattle, WA
	prnts want him to be lawyer
1968	→ interested in computers
	wrote 1st prog – tic tac toe game
1973	grad from h.s.; went to Harvard

🔊 CD 1, TR 18

A Listen to information from the lecture. Circle the letter of the notes that you think create a better time line: *a* or *b*.

a.

```
1998 → Apple intro iMac
   1 yr later – iBook
2001 → iPod (most pop dig music player)
2007 → iPhone (phone = mini comp)
```

b.

```
1998   Apple intro iMac
1999   iBook
2001   iPod
2007   iPhone = mini comp.
```

B Compare your answer with a partner and explain your choice.

Discourse Cues for Chronology Remember to listen for words and phrases that tell you when things happened and the order they happened in. Also, when you listen to a history or a biography (the story of someone's life), listen for dates.

🔊 CD 1, TR 18

C Listen to information from the lecture and write the chronological discourse cues you hear.

1. _____

2. _____

3. _____

4. _____

5. _____

FIRST LISTENING

CD 1, TR 19

Listen to the lecture about Steve Jobs. As you listen, put the following parts of the lecture in the order that you hear them. Number them 1 to 5.

_____ Jobs returned to Apple.

_____ Jobs introduced the iBook.

_____ Jobs began working with Pixar.

_____ Jobs started Apple Computer with Wozniak.

_____ Jobs introduced the "digital hub" strategy.

SECOND LISTENING

CD 1, TR 20

Listen to information from the lecture. The speaker will talk slowly and carefully. You don't have to do anything as you listen. Just relax and listen.

THIRD LISTENING

Listen to the lecture in two parts. Follow the directions for each part. When you have finished, review your notes. Later, you will use them to summarize the lecture with a partner.

Part 1

CD 1, TR 21

You will hear the first part of the lecture again. Listen and complete the notes by adding the abbreviations and symbols from the box.

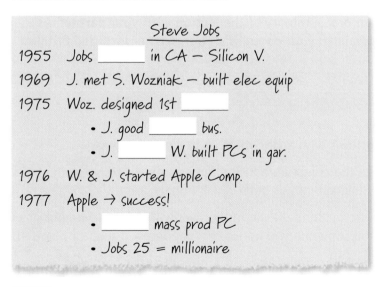

| @ | 1st | PC | b. | & |

Steve Jobs

1955   Jobs _____ in CA — Silicon V.

1969   J. met S. Wozniak — built elec equip

1975   Woz. designed 1st _____

     • J. good _____ bus.

     • J. _____ W. built PCs in gar.

1976   W. & J. started Apple Comp.

1977   Apple → success!

     • _____ mass prod PC

     • Jobs 25 = millionaire

Part 2

CD 1, TR 21

As you listen to the second part of the lecture, take your own notes on a separate piece of paper.

ACCURACY CHECK

🔊 CD 1, TR 22

A You will hear six questions about the lecture. Listen to each question and write the letter of the best answer.

_____ 1. a. 1955
　　 b. 1956
　　 c. 1975
　　 d. 1976

_____ 2. a. 12
　　 b. 14
　　 c. 16
　　 d. 18

_____ 3. a. 20
　　 b. 21
　　 c. 25
　　 d. 27

_____ 4. a. 1955
　　 b. 1975
　　 c. 1985
　　 d. 1995

_____ 5. a. 1978
　　 b. 1988
　　 c. 1998
　　 d. 2008

_____ 6. a. 1951
　　 b. 1971
　　 c. 1991
　　 d. 2011

🔊 CD 1, TR 22

B You will hear four questions about the lecture. Write a short answer to each question. Use your notes.

1. _____

2. _____

3. _____

4. _____

ORAL SUMMARY

Use your notes to create an oral summary of the lecture with your partner. As you work together, add details to your notes that your partner included but you had missed.

DISCUSSION

Discuss the following questions with a classmate or in a small group.

1. What effect do you think the computer and the Internet have had on student life? Name another modern device that has been revolutionary for you.

2. Do you know anyone who might make life in the twenty-first century better or more interesting? Is that person someone you know, or someone you read or heard about?

3. If you were going to spend 10 months alone in a remote area doing research or working on a job, what electronic equipment would you want to have with you? Why?

TASK 1 The Evolution of the Computer

Listen to a short talk about the evolution of computers. As you listen, add the dates to complete the chart below.

Event in Computer Evolution	Date
The abacus was invented in Babylonia.	
Blaise Pascal invented the first automatic calculator. It did not run on electricity; it ran by turning gears and wheels.	
Gottfried Wilhelm Leibniz designed another type of calculator. It also ran with gears and wheels.	
Joseph-Marie Jacquard invented a weaving loom that used punch cards. This led to the coding used in modern computers.	
Charles Babbage invented all of the parts that are used in the modern computer.	
Herman Hollerith invented a calculating machine that counted and sorted information.	
First-generation computers were very large and used vacuum tubes to run.	
Second-generation computers no longer use vacuum tubes. They run on silicon chips.	
Computers became affordable and small enough to fit in a home.	
Computers start to be much like the computers that are in use today.	

TASK 2 Landmarks in Technology

A **Listen to descriptions of people and their companies. As you listen, take notes.**

B **Listen again and answer the questions below. Be ready to do some math to get the right answer!**

1. In what year did Mark Zuckerberg start Facebook? _____

2. In what year did Wikipedia have over 3 million articles? _____

3. In what year did Amazon.com start making profits? _____

4. In what year did Larry Page and Sergey Brin create Google? _____

5. In what year was Bill Gates worth $53 billion? _____

6. In what year was Twitter created? _____

Surviving an Avalanche

BEFORE VIEWING

TOPIC PREVIEW

Look at the photo of an avalanche on this page. Then answer the following questions with a partner.

1. Where do avalanches happen? What causes them?

2. What do you think someone might be doing to get caught in an avalanche?

3. How likely is it for someone to survive an avalanche?

VOCABULARY PREVIEW

Ⓐ Read the definitions of these key words and phrases that you will hear during the video.

snap break suddenly with a short, sharp noise

crushed pressed so hard that something is made flat or broken into pieces

resurfaced came back up to the top

eventually in the end, especially after a long time

unbearable too bad or painful to continue experiencing

hundreds of tons an extreme amount of weight (1 ton = 2,240 lbs or 1,016 kg)

magnitude the size or importance of something

pause stop for a short time

popped right out came out suddenly and forcefully from a small space

B Work with a partner and write in the blank the word or phrase from the box that best completes the sentence.

bottom	flying down	for a moment	fortunately
half	power	showed up	weight

1. As the skier felt the _____ of the avalanche, he **paused** _____ to appreciate the **magnitude** of the event. **Hundreds of tons** of snow were _____ the mountain.

2. The avalanche caused the trees to **snap** in _____.

3. The skier thought he would be **crushed** by the **unbearable** _____ of the snow, but _____ he **popped right out** of the snow.

4. He reached the _____ of the mountain and **resurfaced**, and **eventually** his friends _____.

VIEWING

🖥 FIRST VIEWING

Watch the video, and then compare your first impressions with a partner. Talk about what you remember, what surprised you, and what interested you.

🖥 SECOND VIEWING

Watch the video again. Listen for the missing words and write them in the blanks.

1. The temperatures were _____ pretty significantly so there was a lot of _____ happening in the snow pack.

2. For a moment, actually, I stopped being _____.

3. You don't _____ feel that kind of power ever, especially in an uncontrolled environment.

4. I looked down and I could see the entire avalanche _____, and it was all—I knew I was going to the bottom of the _____.

5. I got to the bottom. I could feel it _____ down, and I popped right out at the toe of the avalanche.

STOP

LAWINENGEFAHR
DANGER D' AVALANCHES

⌨ THIRD VIEWING

Complete these notes as you watch the video. Use abbreviations and symbols as necessary.

```
1) 2 mths ago _____
    • went _____ ft
    • at time was _____ w/_____
2) Watched mtn crack
    • watched trees _____
    • _____ for a while
    • eventually _____
    • thnking never _____
    • for a mo, stop'd _____
3) Back into snow pack
    • _____
    • _____
    • _____
4) 20 mins _____
    • 100% sure _____
    • couldn't _____
```

ORAL SUMMARY

Use your notes to create an oral summary of the video with your partner. As you work together, add details to your notes that your partner included but you had missed.

DISCUSSION

Discuss the following questions with a classmate or in a small group.

1. Jimmy Chin says, "They would have been less surprised if they had been talking to my ghost." What does he mean by this?

2. How do you think Jimmy Chin felt before, during, immediately after, and a few weeks after the avalanche?

3. Jimmy Chin was in what was probably the most frightening situation of his life. What was the scariest situation you have ever experienced? Tell the story.

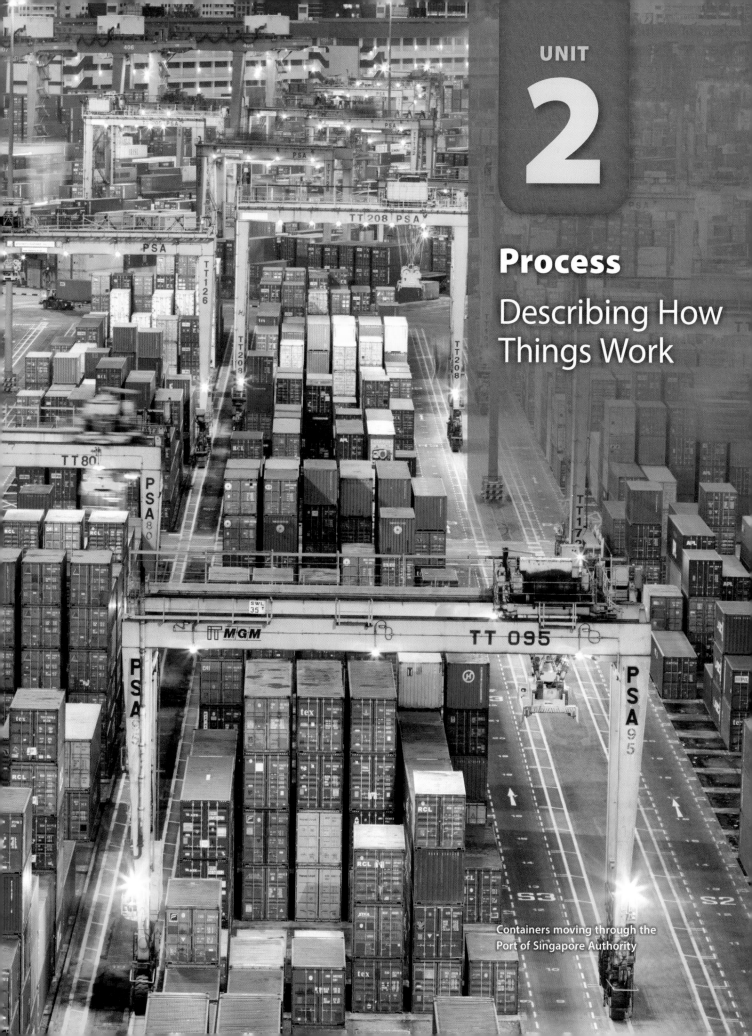

Process

Describing How Things Work

Containers moving through the
Port of Singapore Authority

Roller Coasters

The Ups and Downs of How They Work

TOPIC PREVIEW

Answer the following questions with a partner or your classmates.

1. Have you ever been to an amusement park? If you went to an amusement park today, what kind of ride would you go on? What ride do you think would be the most fun?

2. What kinds of activities do you think little children, young adults, and old people enjoy doing for a day of fun?

3. Why do you think people will pay money to take a roller-coaster ride or do something else that scares them? Give at least two reasons.

Riding a roller coaster at an amusement park in Essen, Germany

VOCABULARY PREVIEW

CD 2, TR 1

A **Listen to the following sentences that contain information from the lecture. As you listen, write the word or phrase from the box that completes the sentence.**

consists of	coming off	gain	gravity	loop
path	physics	sets	slope	

1. Let's talk about the _____ involved in a ride on a roller coaster.

2. A simple roller coaster _____ a frame with a track on it.

3. The track follows a _____ that ends at the same place it started.

4. The roller-coaster cars have two _____ of wheels.

5. The wheels below the track keep the fast-moving cars from _____ the track.

6. At the top of the first hill, the chain comes off the cars and _____ takes over.

7. The cars _____ speed as they roll downhill.

8. Then they go down a very steep _____.

9. The cars travel in a _____ that puts us upside down.

B **Match the words to their definitions.**

_____ 1. loop

_____ 2. come off

_____ 3. slope

_____ 4. gravity

_____ 5. consist of

_____ 6. set

_____ 7. physics

_____ 8. gain

_____ 9. path

a. the force that causes objects to fall to the ground

b. the side of a hill, or a surface that is higher at one end

c. to stop being on or attached to something else

d. to increase in amount

e. to be made up of something

f. a circle made when something curves around and crosses itself

g. a group of things that are similar and are used together

h. the direction or route that something follows

i. the study of energy and matter

PREDICTIONS

Think about the questions in the Topic Preview on page 26 and the sentences you heard in the Vocabulary Preview. Write three questions that you think will be answered in the lecture. Share your questions with your classmates.

NOTETAKING PREPARATION

Steps in a Process

When a speaker describes a process, use numbers in your notes to identify the different steps in the process. Write the name of the process above the numbered steps. Indent the numbered steps.

How ~~~~~~~ ~~~ ~~~~~ ~~
 1. ~~~ ~~ ~~~~ ~~
 2. ~~ ~~~ ~ ~~~~
 3. ~~~~ ~~~
 4. ~~ ~~~~~ ~~~~

A Listen to a brief summary of information from the lecture. Circle the letter of the notes below that best record what you hear.

a.

How roller coasters work
 1. Chain pulls cars ↑ hill
 2. Chain off – g. push ↓ hill v. fast
 3. Bottom – e. to go ↑ next hill

b.

How roller coasters work
 1. Cars go ↑ hill
 2. Grav push cars
 3. Cars go downhill v. fast ↓
 4. Now have eng – go up next hill

B Work with a partner and discuss your choice and why you made it.

Discourse Cues for a Process
When a speaker is describing a process, listen for words and phrases such as the following that signal the steps in the process.

first	then	the first thing that happens is
second	next	during this stage
third	finally	at this point

C Listen to information from the lecture and write the process discourse cues you hear.

1. _____

2. _____

3. _____

4. _____

FIRST LISTENING

CD 2, TR 3

Listen to the lecture on how roller coasters work. As you listen, put the following parts of the lecture in the order that you hear them. Number them 1 to 5.

_____ Start of roller-coaster ride

_____ Summary of the roller-coaster process

_____ The speaker's attitude toward roller coasters

_____ The role of gravity in pushing roller-coaster cars around the track

_____ Description of a simple roller coaster

SECOND LISTENING

CD 2, TR 4

Listen to information from the lecture. The speaker will talk slowly and carefully. You don't have to do anything as you listen. Just relax and listen.

THIRD LISTENING

Listen to the lecture in two parts. Follow the directions for each part. When you have finished, review your notes. Later, you will use them to summarize the lecture with a partner.

Part 1

CD 2, TR 5

You will hear the first part of the lecture again. Listen and complete the notes by adding the abbreviations and symbols from the box.

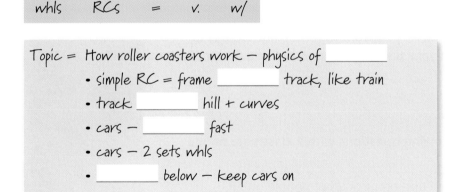

Part 2

CD 2, TR 5

As you listen to the second part of the lecture, take your own notes on a separate piece of paper.

ACCURACY CHECK

CD 2, TR 6

A You will hear six questions about the lecture. Listen to each question and write the letter of the best answer.

_____ 1. a. a frame with a track on it
      b. a structure with wheels on it
      c. a path for workers to walk on
      d. a loop to send the cars around

_____ 2. a. a bicycle
      b. a car
      c. a train
      d. a wagon

_____ 3. a. gravity
      b. energy
      c. speed
      d. chain

_____ 4. a. the track
      b. the cars
      c. gravity
      d. speed

_____ 5. a. biology
      b. physics
      c. chemistry
      d. astronomy

_____ 6. a. Chains stop the cars.
      b. Hills become less steep.
      c. Cars gain energy.
      d. The ride is frightening.

CD 2, TR 6

B You will hear five questions about the lecture. Write a short answer to each question. Use your notes.

1. _____

2. _____

3. _____

4. _____

5. _____

ORAL SUMMARY

Use your notes to create an oral summary of the lecture with your partner. As you work together, add details to your notes that your partner included but you had missed.

DISCUSSION

Discuss the following questions with a classmate or in a small group.

1. Look at the picture on page 26 of people on an amusement park ride. What kind of a ride do you think they are on? Would you go for ride on it? Why or why not?

2. Compare the amusement park ride in the picture on page 26 with the one on this page. What do you think are the differences between them? Which one do you think would be the most thrilling, dangerous, and fun?

3. What role do you think gravity and energy play in the ride in the picture on this page?

TASK 1 Taking a Pulse

🔊
CD 2, TR 7

A **Listen to someone describe how to take a pulse. As you listen, fill in the missing words in the sentences below.**

Taking your pulse is easy. Just follow these _____.
1

First, have a watch with a _____ hand ready or use the
2
stopwatch on your cell phone.

To start with, put the middle three _____ of your
3
right hand on your left wrist just
below your thumb. Press down
a little until you

_____ your pulse
4
beat. Can you feel your pulse?

Look at the second hand on your watch and start _____ the beats that
5
you are feeling with your fingers. _____ 30 seconds, stop counting and
6
write down the _____ of beats that you felt in 30 seconds.
7

Wait a few seconds and then repeat the _____. Write down the
8
second number and _____ it to the first number. This is your
9
pulse _____.
10

B **Have a classmate read the above steps while you take your pulse.**

TASK 2 Yoga Poses

A Make sure that you know the meaning of the following words. Work with a partner and point to these parts of the body.

chin   back   toes   bottom   stomach   knees   forehead

CD 2, TR 8

B Listen to someone describe how to do six different yoga poses. As you listen, match the pictures below with the pose that is described. Write the number of the pose in the box on the picture.

CD 2, TR 8 **C** Listen again and follow the steps to do one of the yoga poses.

Language

How Children Acquire Theirs

TOPIC PREVIEW

Answer the following questions with a partner or your classmates.

1. How do parents and other adults communicate with new babies? And how do new babies let adults know what they want or need?

2. Does a month-old baby who hears only Korean make the same sounds as one who hears English or Russian? Or do these different babies make different languagelike sounds?

3. When do children begin to say words? How do they learn vocabulary and grammar? Do they make mistakes?

A student in Orissa, India

VOCABULARY PREVIEW

CD 2, TR 9

A Listen to the following sentences that contain information from the lecture. As you listen, write the word from the box that completes the sentence.

acquire	babble	backgrounds	cooing
environment	essential	invent	overgeneralize

1. A few weeks after birth, babies start to make _____ noises when they're happy.

2. Around four months of age, babies begin to _____.

3. By 10 months old, the babbling of babies from different language _____ sounds different.

4. At first, babies _____ their own words for things.

5. In the next few months, babies will _____ a lot of words.

6. These words are usually the names of things that are in the baby's

   _____.

7. The speech young children produce is often called "telegraphic" speech because they leave out all but the most _____ words.

8. Babies begin to _____ a grammar rule and make a lot of grammar mistakes.

B Match the words to their definitions.

_____ 1. environment   a. to make something new

_____ 2. essential   b. your family, community, and other things that affect you

_____ 3. acquire   c. the place you usually are and the things in it

_____ 4. coo   d. to gain or learn something

_____ 5. invent   e. to make soft, gentle sounds

_____ 6. background   f. necessary or most important

_____ 7. babble   g. to apply something, such as a rule, at all times

_____ 8. overgeneralize   h. to make speechlike sounds

PREDICTIONS

Think about the questions in the Topic Preview on page 33 and the sentences you heard in the Vocabulary Preview. Write three questions that you think will be answered in the lecture. Share your questions with your classmates.

NOTETAKING PREPARATION

Abbreviating Frequently Repeated Words

When you are listening to a lecture, you will often hear the same words repeated several times. Create special abbreviations for these words in the following ways.

- For the most important word in the lecture, use only the first letter of the word. Make it a capital letter and put a period after it.

    L. = language

- Take out all the vowels in the word.

    bb / bbs = baby / babies

- Use the first few letters of the word.

    ch = children; comm = communication

A Make abbreviations for the following frequently repeated words in the lecture.

1. words _____

2. past tense _____

3. verbs _____

4. acquire / acquisition _____

5. babble / babbling _____

6. first language _____

B Listen to sentences from the lecture and fill in the blanks with abbreviations you created in **A.**

CD 2, TR 10

1. All bbs in world begin _____ ~ same age

2. Next stage of L. _____ begin ~ 18 mths

3. In next mths bbs _____ a lot _____

4. E.g., begin learn rules _____ of _____

5. Think → how is _____ and 2nd _____ diff/sim

Discourse Cues for a Process   Listen for cues that show that a lecturer is going to describe a process. Listen for phrases such as

This is how . . .   *How to . . .*   *The way that . . .*

C Listen to the opening of the lecture and circle the best title for the process that the speaker is going to describe.

CD 2, TR 10

a. How Chldrn Develop

b. How BBs Comm

c. How Chldrn Learn 1st L.

d. How Studs Learn 2nd L.

FIRST LISTENING

CD 2, TR 11

Listen to the lecture on child language development. As you listen, put the following parts of the lecture in the order that you hear them. Number them 1 to 5.

_____ Children make past-tense verb mistakes.

_____ Babies make babbling noises.

_____ Babies use telegraphic speech.

_____ Students are asked to think about first and second language learning processes.

_____ Babies make one-word sentences.

SECOND LISTENING

CD 2, TR 12

Listen to information from the lecture. The speaker will talk slowly and carefully. You don't have to do anything as you listen. Just relax and listen.

THIRD LISTENING

Listen to the lecture in two parts. Follow the directions for each part. When you have finished, review your notes. Later, you will use them to summarize the lecture with a partner.

CD 2, TR 13

Part 1

You will hear the first part of the lecture again. Listen and complete the notes by adding the abbreviations and symbols from the box.

1st	wks	4	mos	diff

How bbs learn 1st L.
    Stage 1
        1. Bbs crying = comm
        2. Few _____ old = cooing
        3. _____ mos = start bbl
        4. 10 _____ = bbl _____ for diff Ls
    Stage 2
        1. _____ wds

CD 2, TR 13

Part 2

As you listen to the second part of the lecture, take your own notes on a separate piece of paper.

ACCURACY CHECK

CD 2, TR 14

You will hear questions and statements about the lecture. For 1–3, listen to the question and write the letter of the best answer. For 4–7, listen to the statement and write *T* for *true* or *F* for *false*.

_____ 1. a. birth
           b. 4 months
           c. 10 months
           d. 18 months

_____ 3. a. 10 to 12 months
           b. 8 to 24 months
           c. 2 to 3 years
           d. 7 to 8 years

_____ 2. a. kiki
           b. Daddy, up.
           c. I walked home.
           d. I goed to bed.

4. _____   5. _____   6. _____   7. _____

ORAL SUMMARY

Use your notes to create an oral summary of the lecture with your partner. As you work together, add details to your notes that your partner included but you had missed.

DISCUSSION

Discuss the following statements with a classmate or in a small group.

1. Parents understand what their baby needs even before the baby begins to talk.

2. It's easy for a baby to learn his or her language, but it's hard work for an adult to learn a second or foreign language.

3. Everyone should learn to speak the dominant language of the country where they live even if a different language is spoken in their home.

4. It would be better if everybody in the world spoke the same language.

TASK 1 Stages in Language Development

🔊 CD 2, TR 15

A Listen to these English-speaking babies and children. Write down what you hear each one say.

1. _____
2. _____
3. _____
4. _____
5. _____

B Compare your answers in **A** with a partner. Discuss the meaning of what each baby said.

🔊 CD 2, TR 15

C Listen again. Draw a line to match the speech of each child, 1 to 5, to a stage of language development that you learned about in the lecture. The first one is done for you.

1   Babbling

2   One-word speech

3   Telegraphic speech

4   Overgeneralize past tense

5   Multiword speech

TASK 2 Writing an E-mail

🔊 CD 2, TR 16

A Listen and write down the five tips, or steps, in writing effective e-mail messages. You will hear each tip twice.

1. _____
2. _____
3. _____
4. _____
5. _____

B Check your answers with a partner. Then, with your partner, decide on one or two more rules that you think would be helpful.

CHAPTER 6

Robots

How They Work and Learn to Work

TOPIC PREVIEW

Answer the following questions with a partner or your classmates.

1. What do you picture when you think of "a robot"? What does it look like? What does it do? Draw a simple picture of your robot.

2. Have you seen a movie or TV show in which robots play an important role? What was the name of the movie? What did the robots do in the movie? How do "real" robots differ from "movie" robots?

3. What will robots look like and be doing in 10 years? in 20 years? in 50 years?

A student builds a robot.

VOCABULARY PREVIEW

🔊
CD 3, TR 1

Ⓐ **Listen to the following sentences that contain information from the lecture. As you listen, write the word from the box that completes the sentence.**

assembly	autonomous	detect	efficiently	guidance
industrial	precise	repetitive	sensors	stores

1. Today, I'm going to talk mostly about _____ robots.

2. These robots do work that is _____, dangerous, or boring.

3. The robot learns to do its job with the _____ of a human being.

4. Robotic arms on the _____ line join the parts of a car together.

5. Robots are very _____ when repeating a task.

6. Robots do work humans could do, but they do it more _____.

7. The robot _____ the exact movements in its computer memory.

8. A robot uses _____ to gather information.

9. An _____ machine can change its behavior in relation to its surroundings.

10. Honda's ASIMO can _____ the movements of people nearby.

Ⓑ **Match the words to their definitions.**

_____ 1. detect a. over and over in the same way each time

_____ 2. precise b. used in industry and manufacturing

_____ 3. autonomous c. a device that reacts to change in light, heat, sound, etc.

_____ 4. industrial d. to save information to be used again

_____ 5. store e. to find or become aware of something

_____ 6. repetitive f. help, assistance, and direction

_____ 7. guidance g. the process of putting something together

_____ 8. assembly h. done quickly and correctly

_____ 9. sensor i. accurate and correct

_____ 10. efficiently j. independent; able to act alone

PREDICTIONS

Think about the questions in the Topic Preview on page 39 and the sentences you heard in the Vocabulary Preview. Write three questions that you think will be answered in the lecture. Share your questions with your classmates.

NOTETAKING PREPARATION

Listening for New Sections of a Lecture

Different sections of a lecture deal with different aspects of the lecturer's chosen topic. As you listen to a lecture, listen for when the lecturer moves from one aspect of the topic to a new aspect. When that happens, leave a space and start a new section in your notes.

A section of a lecture may, for example, give a definition, provide historical background, analyze reasons, or describe a process.

A lecturer will use language such as the following to introduce a new section:

I'd like to start by defining . . .
Now, let's talk about why . . .
So what is the process by which . . .
Next, I want to examine the history of . . .

A Listen to three section openings from the lecture. Take notes.

CD 3, TR 2

1.

2.

3.

B Listen again to the section openings from the lecture. Circle what you think the lecturer will go on to talk about in each section.

CD 3, TR 2

1. a. historical background   b. a process   c. a description   d. a definition

2. a. historical background   b. a process   c. a description   d. a definition

3. a. historical background   b. a process   c. a description   d. a definition

Discourse Cues for a Process   When you listen to steps in a process, remember to listen for language that signals the different steps. Review the discourses cues on pages 28 and 35.

C Listen to sentences from the lecture. Write the cue you hear in each sentence that shows the lecturer is describing a step in a process.

CD 3, TR 2

1. _____   4. _____

2. _____   5. _____

3. _____

FIRST LISTENING

CD 3, TR 3

Listen to the lecture on robots. As you listen, put the following parts of the lecture in the order that you hear them. Number them 1 to 5.

_____ How robots learn their job

_____ Robots more effective than humans

_____ An example of an autonomous machine

_____ Automatic robots

_____ Robots on factory assembly lines

SECOND LISTENING

CD 3, TR 4

Listen to information from the lecture. The speaker will talk slowly and carefully. You don't have to do anything as you listen. Just relax and listen.

THIRD LISTENING

Listen to the lecture in two parts. Follow the directions for each part. When you have finished, review your notes. Later, you will use them to summarize the lecture with a partner.

CD 3, TR 5

Part 1

You will hear the first part of the lecture again. Listen and complete the notes by adding the abbreviations and symbols from the box.

| machs | e.g. | contr | Rs | = |

1) what robots lk like
   - not humans
   - _____

2) today's topic _____ Indust Rs
   - Rs do wk — rep, dang, boring
   - most _____ wk in factories, _____ ptg lids on jars
   - in car facts Rs — very precise
   - Rs do human wk more effic'ly and precisely

3) how rbts wk
   - rbts 1st need _____ syst

CD 3, TR 5

Part 2

As you listen to the second part of the lecture, take your own notes on a separate piece of paper.

ACCURACY CHECK

CD 3, TR 6

A You will hear six questions about the lecture. Listen to each question and write the letter of the best answer.

_____ 1. a. easy
　　　 b. human
　　　 c. repetitive
　　　 d. interesting

_____ 2. a. jars of fruit
　　　 b. parts of cars
　　　 c. wheels on tires
　　　 d. bolts on wheels

_____ 3. a. sensor
　　　 b. power
　　　 c. control system
　　　 d. arms and legs

_____ 4. a. an automatic robot
　　　 b. an industrial machine
　　　 c. a handheld computer
　　　 d. its brain

_____ 5. a. with the guidance of a human being
　　　 b. with the help of another robot
　　　 c. with its arms and hands
　　　 d. with its moving parts

_____ 6. a. find it
　　　 b. lift and move it
　　　 c. determine its weight
　　　 d. determine the amount of force to use

CD 3, TR 6

B You will hear four questions about the lecture. Write a short answer to each question. Use your notes.

1. _____
2. _____
3. _____
4. _____

ORAL SUMMARY

Use your notes to create an oral summary of the lecture with your partner. As you work together, add details to your notes that your partner included but you had missed.

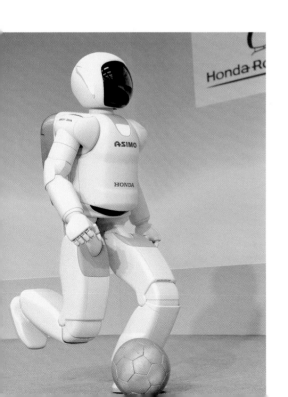

DISCUSSION

Discuss the following questions with a classmate or in a small group.

1. Robots do many jobs in factories that people used to do. What are some of the reasons why robots are now used for these jobs? Do robots put people out of work?

2. Robots will continue to become more humanlike until they look, talk, and think much like human beings. Is this a good thing or a bad thing? Why?

3. 3-D printers already exist. In the future similar machines could use nanobots—robots too small to see—to turn raw materials into new products. Is this a good idea? Why?

TASK 1 Steps in Doing Research

CD 3, TR 7

A **Listen to someone describe the steps in doing research. As you listen, match the steps below to the pictures. Write the number of the step next to the picture.**

Step 1: Do background research.

Step 2: Conduct your experiment.

Step 3: Make observations.

Step 4: Record and analyze your results.

Step 5: Present your research.

Step _____

Step _____

Step _____

Step _____

Step _____

B **Compare your answers with a partner and explain your choices.**

TASK 2 A Simple Experiment

A Listen to things you will need to perform a simple experiment. Write each one next to its picture.

CD 3, TR 8

B Listen to the description of the experiment. As you listen, fill in the missing words in the sentences below.

CD 3, TR 8

First, pour some _____ into the bottle until it is about one-

_____ full. Next, use the _____ to pour some baking soda
_____2_____   _____3_____

into the _____. After _____, carefully stretch the balloon
              _____4_____   _____5_____

over the _____ of the bottle. Make sure you don't _____ any
              _____6_____   _____7_____

baking _____ into the bottle! Next, _____ up the heavy part
              _____8_____   _____9_____

of the balloon so that the baking soda _____ into the bottle.
                                                      _____10_____

C Work with a partner. Talk about what you think will happen next.

D Listen to the description of the end of the experiment. Was your guess correct?

CD 3, TR 8

Tristan da Cunha Oil Spill

BEFORE VIEWING

TOPIC PREVIEW

Work with a partner and describe the picture on this page. Discuss how this happened and what steps people will take now to help the birds and their environment. Write the steps below.

VOCABULARY PREVIEW

A Read the definitions of these key words and phrases that you will hear during the video.

remotest farthest away from places where people live

inhabited having people living in or on it

devastating causing a lot of damage or destruction

endangered likely to be harmed or damaged, and possibly die and disappear

transmit images send photos or videos

off the grid not connected to public energy or communication networks

got picked up was reported on by a newspaper or a news program

got it out made sure people heard about it

capturing recording events, usually with photographs or video

B Work with a partner and write vocabulary from **A** in the blanks in the sentences.

1. Tristan da Cunha, one of the _____ islands in the world, is _____ by fewer than 300 people.

2. The island is outside the area of a satellite signal and, therefore, _____.

3. _____ a news event on camera when it happens is the goal of every news photographer.

4. They were able to _____ of the _____ destruction even though they were in the middle of the Pacific Ocean.

5. The birds on the island were an _____ species.

6. Andrew Evans' story _____ by the news media very quickly, but it was *National Geographic* that first _____ to the public.

VIEWING

🖵 FIRST VIEWING

Watch the video, and then compare your first impressions with a partner. Talk about what you remember, what surprised you, and what interested you.

🖵 SECOND VIEWING

Watch the video again. Listen for the missing words and write them in the blanks.

1. It was a big _____ spill that affected a lot of Northern Rock Hopper Penguins.

2. This is an _____ that's completely disconnected. It's off the grid.

3. But _____ are important because they're organic.

4. They published it. They got it _____ there in the real press.

5. This is something that _____ of you can do and _____ of you are doing all the time.

A boat sinks off the coast of Tristan da Cunha, spilling oil.

Complete these notes as you watch the video. Write only important words, not full sentences, and abbreviate common words.

1) Arr. T. da C. — saw _____
   • devastating
   • affect. pengs — _____
2) Alone there — no comm w/_____
3) Steps A.E. took
   1. took pics
   2. _____ vid.
   3. pub it
   4. + _____
   5. Tweeted it
   6. put on _____
   7. N.G. _____
   8. N.Y.T. _____
4) All of you can
   _____
   _____

ORAL SUMMARY

Use your notes to create an oral summary of the video with your partner. As you work together, add details to your notes that your partner included but you had missed.

DISCUSSION

Discuss the following questions with a classmate or in a small group.

1. In the video, you see a newspaper headline "You Really Shouldn't Crash Your Oil Tanker Where a National Geographic Photographer Is." Explain this headline.

2. Andrew Evans suggests that today with our cell phones and the Internet, we can all be reporters. What are some dangers of the general public spreading news this way?

3. Have you ever witnessed a newsworthy event while it happened? Did you or anyone you were with communicate it to others in any way to "get the news out"?

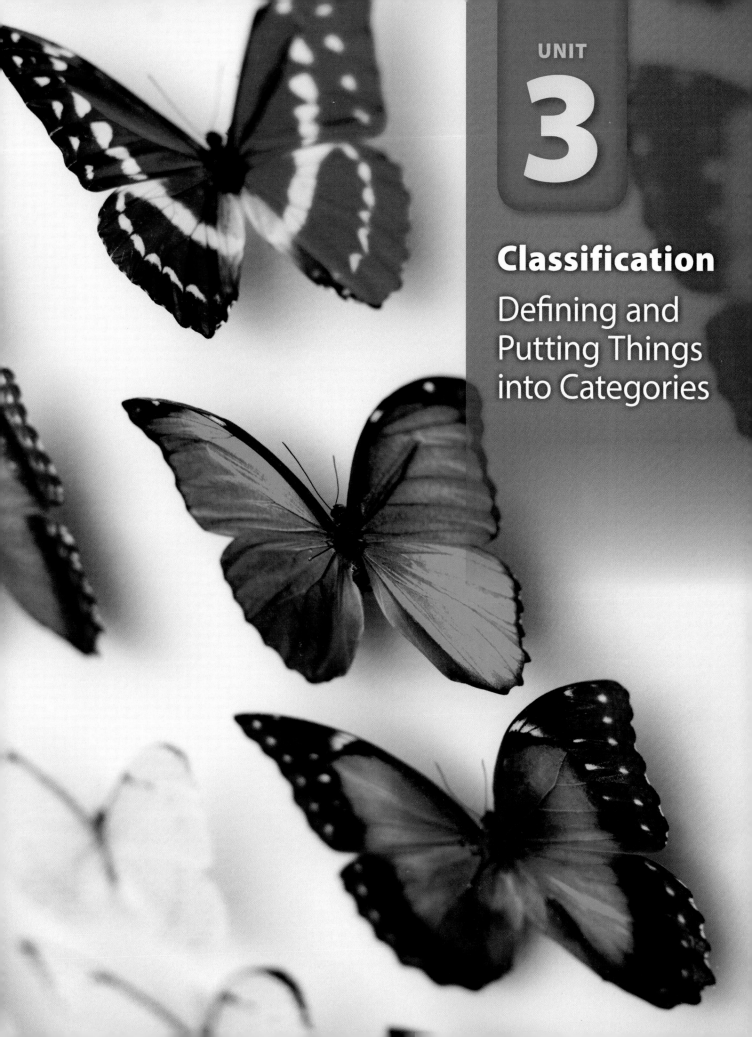

Classification

Defining and Putting Things into Categories

A Tidal Wave

What Is It? Can We Predict It?

TOPIC PREVIEW

Answer the following questions with a partner or your classmates.

1. Have you ever experienced an earthquake, a volcano, or a terrible storm? Describe the experience. What happened? What did you do? How did you survive?

2. What is the difference between a tidal wave and a normal ocean wave? What causes each one?

3. Where and when have there been large earthquakes and tidal waves in recent years? What happened? How destructive were they?

A tsunami pours into the city of Miyako, Japan, March 11, 2011.

VOCABULARY PREVIEW

CD 3, TR 9

A Listen to the following sentences that contain information from the lecture. As you listen, write the word from the box that completes the sentence.

crisis	destructive	massive	merging	predict
rushing	shifts	storms	trembles	warn

1. A tidal wave is a very large and _____ wall of water.

2. A tidal wave comes _____ in suddenly and unexpectedly at any time.

3. Do you know that tidal waves are not caused by _____?

4. When an earthquake takes place under the ocean, the ocean floor shakes and _____.

5. Sometimes the ocean floor _____ during an underwater earthquake.

6. A double-wave tsunami can also be called a _____ tsunami.

7. In 2011, a _____ earthquake occurred off the coast of Japan.

8. A tsunami caused a _____ at a nuclear plant in northeastern Japan.

9. Today scientists can _____ that a tidal wave will hit land.

10. It is possible to _____ people that a tidal wave is coming.

B Match the words to their definitions.

_____ 1. crisis   a. to mix two or more things together into one

_____ 2. destructive   b. to change position

_____ 3. merge   c. a very difficult or dangerous situation

_____ 4. predict   d. to tell someone of a possible problem or danger

_____ 5. rush   e. causing or able to cause serious damage

_____ 6. shift   f. to say that a particular thing will happen

_____ 7. massive   g. bad weather with a lot of wind
                            and rain or snow

_____ 8. storm
                         h. to shake from side to side
_____ 9. tremble
                         i. extremely large
_____ 10. warn
                         j. to move very quickly

PREDICTIONS

Think about the questions in the Topic Preview on page 50 and the sentences you heard in the Vocabulary Preview. Write three questions that you think will be answered in the lecture. Share your questions with your classmates.

TSUNAMI EVACUATION ROUTE

NOTETAKING PREPARATION

Recording Definitions

In a talk, it is sometimes necessary for the speaker to define some of the terms used in the lecture. Usually the lecturer will give a *positive* definition, that is, the speaker will tell you what something is or what it means. Sometimes, however, a speaker may give a *negative* definition and tell you what something is not or what it does *not* mean.

When taking notes, the following symbols are useful abbreviations for showing positive and negative definitions:

Positive definition $=$

Negative definition $\neq$

A tidal wave is a destructive wall of water   TW = destr wall H$_2$O

🔊 CD 3, TR 10

A **Listen to the following positive and negative definitions of terms used in the lecture. Use either the symbol = or ≠ to complete the notes below.**

1. TW _____ a wave ← tide

2. tsunami _____ TW

3. double tsunami _____ 2 TWs together

4. v. big waves at sea _____ TWs

Discourse Cues for Definition and Classification   Listen for words and phrases that tell you the lecturer is giving you a definition. These are some cues that the lecturer may use to define a term:

is/are (known as) . . .   *can be defined as* . . .
is a type of . . .   *means* . . .

🔊 CD 3, TR 10

B **Listen to the definitions of some terms in the lecture. As you listen, write the word or phrase from the box that completes the definition.**

means	can be defined as	is a type of	is

1. A tidal wave _____ a very large and destructive wave.

2. To quake _____ to move up and down very quickly or to shake.

3. A true tide _____ the normal rise and fall of ocean water at regular times each day.

4. A seismograph _____ instrument for measuring earthquakes.

FIRST LISTENING
CD 3, TR 11

Listen to the lecture on tidal waves. As you listen, put the following parts of the lecture in the order that you hear them. Number them 1 to 5.

____ Predicting earthquakes

____ The tsunami of March 2011

____ An overview of the lecture

____ Definition of a tidal wave

____ Cause of tidal waves

SECOND LISTENING
CD 3, TR 12

Listen to information from the lecture. The speaker will talk slowly and carefully. You don't have to do anything as you listen. Just relax and listen.

THIRD LISTENING

Listen to the lecture in two parts. Follow the directions for each part. When you have finished, review your notes. Later, you will use them to summarize the lecture with a partner.

Part 1
CD 3, TR 13

You will hear the first part of the lecture again. Listen and complete the notes by adding the abbreviations and symbols from the box.

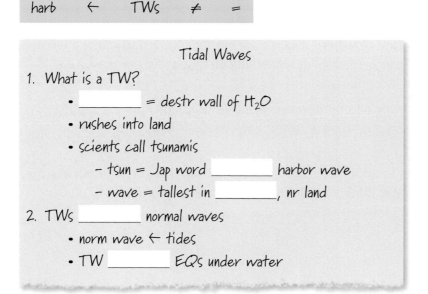

| harb | ← | TWs | ≠ | = |

Tidal Waves

1. What is a TW?
   - _____ = destr wall of H_2O
   - rushes into land
   - scients call tsunamis
     - tsun = Jap word _____ harbor wave
     - wave = tallest in _____, nr land
2. TWs _____ normal waves
   - norm wave ← tides
   - TW _____ EQs under water

Part 2
CD 3, TR 13

As you listen to the second part of the lecture, take your own notes on a separate piece of paper.

CD 3, TR 14

ACCURACY CHECK

You will hear eight questions about the lecture. Listen to each question and choose the correct answer from the box and write it on the line.

double-wave tsunami	harbor	harbor wave	ocean floor
seismograph	tidal wave	tide	wall of water

1. _____

2. _____

3. _____

4. _____

5. _____

6. _____

7. _____

8. _____

ORAL SUMMARY

Use your notes to create an oral summary of the lecture with your partner. As you work together, add details to your notes that your partner included but you had missed.

DISCUSSION

Discuss the following questions with a classmate or in a small group.

1. What is the worst kind of natural disaster: an earthquake, a hurricane, a wildfire, a tidal wave, a volcano eruption, or something else? Explain the reason for your choice.

2. Which of the following natural disasters is easiest to predict: an earthquake, a hurricane, a tornado, a tidal wave, a volcano eruption? Explain the reason for your choice.

3. Do you know what to do if there is an earthquake, a hurricane, a flood, or a tornado? What do you think you should do if one of them happened?

TASK 1 Listening for Definitions

CD 3, TR 15

A Listen to the clues and write the words in the spaces in the crossword puzzle. The clues are definitions. The first answer, 1 across, will be given to you.

CD 3, TR 15

B Listen to the crossword puzzle answers. Check your answers and fill in any that you missed.

TASK 2 Natural Disasters
CD 3, TR 16

Listen to a description of four natural disasters and fill in the missing information in the chart.

Category of Disaster by Cause	Event	Location	Date of Event	Approximate Number of Casualties
Geological	landslide		1958	
Meteorological		Bangladesh		1,300 people
Hydrological			1887	
Space	asteroid explosion			

8

Levels of Language

Formal and Informal

TOPIC PREVIEW

Answer the following questions with a partner or your classmates.

1. Have you ever said something in English, and the person you were speaking with looked at you with surprise or confusion? What kind of mistake did you make?

2. When you meet your friend's mother, is it more correct to say, "Hi, Jennifer" or "Hello, Mrs. Collier"? Why do you think your choice is the right one?

3. If you were talking to a friend about a teacher you like, would you be more likely to say, "Jones is a great teacher" or "Doctor Jones is a truly great educator"? Explain your choice.

Friends chat as sand blows around them in the Libyan desert.

VOCABULARY PREVIEW

CD 4, TR 1

A Listen to the following sentences that contain information from the lecture. As you listen, write the word from the box that completes the sentence.

| authority | ceremonies | colleagues | interacting |
| polite | reference | tend | usage |

1. Today I want to talk about levels of language _____.

2. Formal written language is the kind you find in _____ books such as encyclopedias.

3. People usually use formal English at _____ such as graduations.

4. We also _____ to use formal language in conversations with persons we don't know well.

5. Formal language tends to be more _____.

6. Informal language is used in conversation with _____, family, and friends.

7. I might say to a friend, "Close the door, please." To someone in _____ I would say, "Excuse me, could you please close the door?"

8. The difference between formal and informal usage can be learned by observing and _____ with native speakers.

B Match the words to their definitions.

_____ 1. ceremony   a. containing facts and other information

_____ 2. colleague   b. to usually happen or to be likely to happen

_____ 3. authority   c. to talk to other people when doing
                              something together
_____ 4. interact
                           d. a formal event on a special occasion
_____ 5. usage
                           e. behaving in a way that shows respect for others
_____ 6. reference
                           f. the power or responsibility to make decisions
_____ 7. tend
                           g. a person you work with
_____ 8. polite
                           h. the way words are used

PREDICTIONS

Think about the questions in the Topic Preview on page 56 and the sentences you heard in the Vocabulary Preview. Write three questions that you think will be answered in the lecture. Share your questions with your classmates.

NOTETAKING PREPARATION

Listening for Examples

A good lecturer will always make concepts clearer by providing good examples. Listen for language that tells you that the lecturer is going to introduce an example, such as the following:

For example   *Let me illustrate*
For instance   *Such as*
Let me give you an example

When you hear an example, write the example below the concept that is being defined and indent your notes. Many notetakers introduce the example with one of these abbreviations:

e.g.
ex.

🔊 CD 4, TR 2

A **Listen to a part of the lecture while you look at the notes below. After you listen, rewrite the notes in a clearer notetaking format.**

Diff betwn form & inform vocab
When talkng to friend
ex. — use crazy about
w/boss use really enjoy

Discourse Cues for Definition and Classification Listen for cues that show the lecturer is going to give an example. Make sure you include the example in your notes. This will help you understand the lecture.

🔊 CD 4, TR 2

B **Listen to five sentences that contain information from the lecture. As you listen, write the language cue in each sentence that the lecturer uses to introduce an example.**

1. _____
2. _____
3. _____
4. _____
5. _____

CD 4, TR 3

FIRST LISTENING

Listen to the lecture on formal and informal language. As you listen, put the following parts of the lecture in the order that you hear them. Number them 1 to 5.

_____ Differences in vocabulary used in formal and informal language

_____ Tips for a nonnative speaker learning English to learn formal and informal language

_____ Differences in polite phrases used in formal and informal language

_____ Definition and examples of formal language

_____ All languages use different words and phrases in different situations

CD 4, TR 4

SECOND LISTENING

Listen to information from the lecture. The speaker will talk slowly and carefully. You don't have to do anything as you listen. Just relax and listen.

THIRD LISTENING

Listen to the lecture in two parts. Follow the directions for each part. When you have finished, review your notes. Later, you will use them to summarize the lecture with a partner.

Part 1

CD 4, TR 5

You will hear the first part of the lecture again. Listen and complete the notes by adding the abbreviations and symbols from the box.

ex	inform	=	etc.	sits

Levels of Lang Use
1. All langs — two cats _____ form and inform lvls
   • Diff from correct vs incorrect
   • = diff for diff _____
2. form = txtbks, ref books _____
        ex letter to univ, essays, lectures etc.
        _____ conv w/profs etc
3. _____ lang = conv w/ friends + pers notes etc.

Part 2

CD 4, TR 5

As you listen to the second part of the lecture, take your own notes on a separate piece of paper.

ACCURACY CHECK

CD 4, TR 6

You will hear questions and statements about the lecture. For 1–4, listen to the question and write the letter of the best answer. For 5–8, listen to the statement and write *T* for *true* or *F* for *false*.

_____ 1. a. e-mail to friends
   b. essays
   c. personal notes
   d. text messages

_____ 2. a. family
   b. friends
   c. teammates
   d. all of the above

_____ 3. a. Salt, please.
   b. Pass the salt.
   c. Pass the salt, please.
   d. Could you please pass the salt?

_____ 4. a. I enjoy music.
   b. I saw the cops.
   c. I admire Greek culture.
   d. None of the above

5. _____   6. _____   7. _____   8. _____

ORAL SUMMARY

Use your notes to create an oral summary of the lecture with your partner. As you work together, add details to your notes that your partner included but you had missed.

DISCUSSION

Discuss the following questions with a classmate or in a small group.

1. Is it better to speak formal English in all situations? Why or why not?

2. When you begin learning a second language, should you first learn formal language or informal language? Why?

3. What are some of the ways you think young children learn to use formal and informal language?

4. In what ways do you think it is difficult or easy for second language learners to learn the difference between formal and informal usage?

TASK 1 Homonyms and Homophones

A *homonym* is a word that is spelled and pronounced the same as another word but has a different meaning, for example *right* (correct) and *right* (opposite of left).

A *homophone* is a word that is spelled differently from another word but pronounced the same, for example *write* and *right*.

CD 4, TR 7

A Listen to two sentences. One word sounds the same in each sentence. Decide if the word is a *homonym* or a *homophone*, and put a check (✓) in the column. The first one is done for you.

	Homonym	Homophone
1.	_____	✓
2.	_____	_____
3.	_____	_____
4.	_____	_____
5.	_____	_____
6.	_____	_____
7.	_____	_____
8.	_____	_____
9.	_____	_____

CD 4, TR 7

B Listen to the sentences again. This time write the two words. The first one is done for you.

	First sentence	Second sentence
1.	won	one
2.	_____	_____
3.	_____	_____
4.	_____	_____
5.	_____	_____
6.	_____	_____
7.	_____	_____
8.	_____	_____
9.	_____	_____

🔊
CD 4, TR 8

TASK 2 Classifying Parts of Speech

Listen to descriptions of the classification of different types of words. As you hear the examples, fill in the charts below.

1.

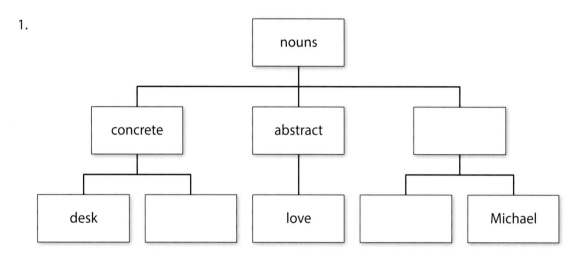

2.

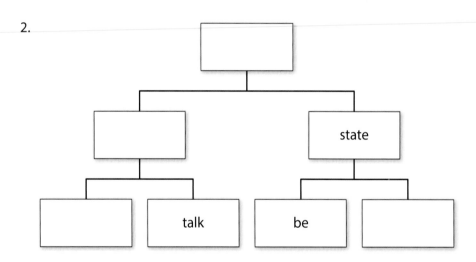

3.

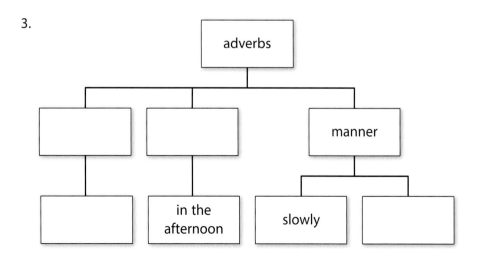

Power

The Kinds of Power People Use and Abuse

TOPIC PREVIEW

Answer the following questions with a partner or your classmates.

1. Who has power over you in your life? What gives these people power?

2. Who do you have power over? What kind of power is it?

3. What gives people power? Some possible sources of power are physical strength, knowledge, wealth, and political influence. Give examples of people you know of who have a lot of each kind of power.

Prince of the Kingdom of Toro, Uganda

VOCABULARY PREVIEW

🔊
CD 4, TR 9

A Listen to the following sentences that contain information from the lecture. As you listen, write the word or phrase from the box that completes the sentence.

admires	coercive	expertise	identify with	imitate
legitimate	manipulate	referent	uncomfortable	

1. We all wish to avoid _____ emotions.

2. People who have information can _____ those who do not have this information.

3. Some people may _____ a particular friend or, say, a rock star.

4. Many people _____ and are controlled by the people they identify with.

5. _____ power can be used for good or evil purposes.

6. Often a person _____ or wants to behave like a particular person.

7. Government officials usually exercise _____ power.

8. Some experts use their _____ to gain power.

9. Reward or _____ power is used to reward or punish people's actions or behavior.

B Match the words to their definitions.

_____ 1. legitimate

_____ 2. expertise

_____ 3. manipulate

_____ 4. admire

_____ 5. referent

_____ 6. coercive

_____ 7. identify with

_____ 8. imitate

_____ 9. uncomfortable

a. nervous and not relaxed

b. acceptable and legal

c. to make people do what you want, often without them knowing it

d. to like and respect someone

e. to copy the way someone acts

f. knowledge and skill

g. something or someone that you refer to

h. to feel that you understand and are like another person

i. using force to persuade someone to do something

PREDICTIONS

Think about the questions in the Topic Preview on page 63 and the sentences you heard in the Vocabulary Preview. Write three questions that you think will be answered in the lecture. Share your questions with your classmates.

NOTETAKING PREPARATION

Listening for Classifying Language

During a talk or a lecture, a speaker may define a concept by dividing it into various classes or categories. Listen for language that signals that a lecturer is using categories, such as the following:

	several	categories		
	two	types		
There are	three	kinds		of **X**.
	etc.	sorts		
		classes		

	consists of	several	main	categories.
X	comprises	two		types.
	is made up of	three		

As the lecturer describes each type or category, make sure that you write a number for each new type. Also, leave a space between the notes for each new type.

CD 4, TR 10

A Listen to five sentences from the lecture. Match the notes below to the information you hear. Write the number of the sentence in the blank.

_____ P. = 5 cats

_____ 2 more classes of P. – ref & legit

_____ 1st type of P. = inf P.

_____ exp P. = 1+ var of P.

_____ 5th type of P. = reward or coerc P.

Discourse Cues for Definition and Classification   After a lecturer has told you that there are several different kinds of something, listen for the language that tells you that the lecturer is moving from one kind to a new kind.

CD 4, TR 10

B Listen to sentences that contain information from the lecture. As you listen, write down the missing words from each sentence.

1. The _____ _____ of power is reward power.

2. _____ _____ of power is referent power.

3. A _____ _____ of power is classified as legitimate power.

4. The _____ _____ of power is expert power.

5. The _____ _____ of power is information power.

◀» FIRST LISTENING

CD 4, TR 11

Listen to the lecture on types of power. As you listen, put the following parts of the lecture in the order that you hear them. Number them 1 to 5.

_____ Referent power

_____ Reward or coercive power

_____ Information power

_____ Expert power

_____ Legitimate power

◀» SECOND LISTENING

CD 4, TR 12

Listen to information from the lecture. The speaker will talk slowly and carefully. You don't have to do anything as you listen. Just relax and listen.

THIRD LISTENING

Listen to the lecture in two parts. Follow the directions for each part. When you have finished, review your notes. Later, you will use them to summarize the lecture with a partner.

◀» **Part 1**

CD 4, TR 13

You will hear the first part of the lecture again. Listen and complete the notes by adding the abbreviations and symbols from the box.

| e.g. | def | → | legit | 5 |

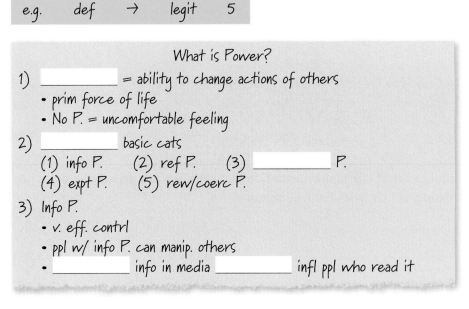

What is Power?
1) _____ = ability to change actions of others
   • prim force of life
   • No P. = uncomfortable feeling
2) _____ basic cats
   (1) info P.   (2) ref P.   (3) _____ P.
   (4) expt P.   (5) rew/coerc P.
3) Info P.
   • v. eff. contrl
   • ppl w/ info P. can manip. others
   • _____ info in media _____ infl ppl who read it

◀» **Part 2**

CD 4, TR 13

As you listen to the second part of the lecture, take your own notes on a separate piece of paper.

CD 4, TR 14

ACCURACY CHECK

You will hear questions and statements about the lecture. For 1–4, listen to the question and write the letter of the best answer. For 5–9, listen to the statement and write *T* for *true* or *F* for *false*.

_____ 1. a. reward
    b. referent
    c. legitimate
    d. information

_____ 3. a. coercive
    b. referent
    c. legitimate
    d. information

_____ 2. a. reward
    b. referent
    c. legitimate
    d. information

_____ 4. a. expert
    b. referent
    c. legitimate
    d. information

5. _____   6. _____   7. _____   8. _____   9. _____

ORAL SUMMARY

Use your notes to create an oral summary of the lecture with your partner. As you work together, add details to your notes that your partner included but you had missed.

DISCUSSION

Discuss the following questions with a classmate or in a small group.

1. To some people, power is a game in which winners are powerful, and losers are powerless. Do you agree this statement? Explain why.

2. What types of people have referent power? For example, do rock stars, movie stars, and parents have referent power? Why?

3. Do you agree with the idea that information power is the most effective type of personal power? Explain why.

4. Would you say that governments that use reward or coercive power over their people use this power for good? Can you give any examples?

TASK 1 Classifying Animals

🔊
CD 4, TR 15

A Listen to these definitions of classes of animal. As you listen, complete the chart below.

	Mammal	Bird	Fish	Reptile	Amphibian
Warm-blooded	✓				
Cold-blooded					
Lives on land	✓				
Lives in water	✓				
Has two legs and wings					
Has fins					
Gets oxygen from air	✓				
Gets oxygen from water					
Starts life in water, but can live on land					
Feeds milk to its young from mother's body	✓				
All or most lay eggs					

B Compare your answers with a partner.

TASK 2 What's That Animal?

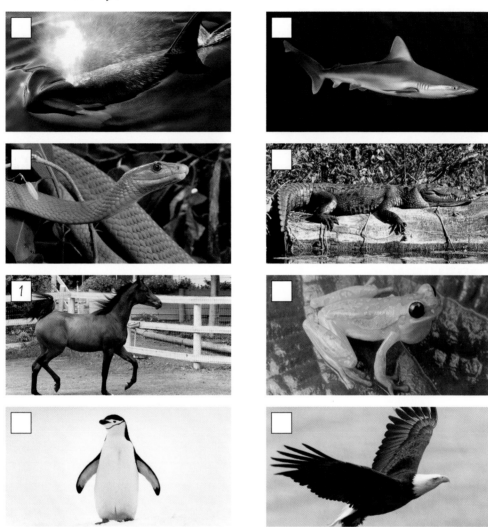

A **Listen to descriptions of animals. As you listen, match the description to a picture of the animal and write the number in the box on the picture. The first one is done for you.**

B **Listen to the name and spelling of each animal and its class, and write them below.**

1. Animal: _____horse_____ Class: _____mammal_____

2. Animal: _____ Class: _____

3. Animal: _____ Class: _____

4. Animal: _____ Class: _____

5. Animal: _____ Class: _____

6. Animal: _____ Class: _____

7. Animal: _____ Class: _____

8. Animal: _____ Class: _____

People, Plants, and Pollinators

BEFORE VIEWING

TOPIC PREVIEW

Write down five things that you think about bees. Then compare your list with a classmate's list.

_____

_____

_____

_____

_____

VOCABULARY PREVIEW

A Read the definitions of these key words and phrases that you will hear during the video.

entomologist a scientist who studies insects

originate to come from

migrated in waves moved in large groups from one area to another

diversity the fact of there being many different forms or varieties

gentle having a kind or quiet nature; not violent

species a group of plants or animals that share many similar qualities

beekeeper a person who raises bees

valuable worth a lot of money

pollinate to take pollen from a male plant to a female plant

crops plants that are grown in large quantities by farmers

B Work with a partner and guess whether the following statements are true or false. Write *T* for *true* or *F* for *false*.

_____ 1. Dino Martins is an **entomologist**.

_____ 2. Bees **originated** in South America and then **migrated in waves** to the rest of the world.

_____ 3. There is very little **diversity** in honeybees. They are all very similar.

_____ 4. Honeybees can be very **gentle** insects.

_____ 5. **Beekeepers** only ever keep one **species** of bees at a time.

_____ 6. Some varieties of honey are more **valuable** than others.

_____ 7. **Crops**, such as chocolate and coffee, need insects to **pollinate** them.

🖥 FIRST VIEWING

Watch the video. As you watch, check your answers in B, above. Then discuss with a partner why each statement is *true* or *false*.

🖥 SECOND VIEWING

Watch the video again. Listen for the missing words and write them in the blanks.

1. There are two fantastic varieties of honeybee that we get to work with, the lovely mountain honeybee, Monticola, which is a very gentle, _____-colored species and produces lots and lots of _____.

2. And Maria here is a beekeeper, a _____ beekeeper on the slopes of Mount Meru in Tanzania. And you can see a view inside the stingless _____ there.

3. A lot of the work I'm trying to develop right now is managing and _____ stingless bee.

4. He even keeps species that _____ don't know about.

5. If you can spend just _____ minutes a day in the company of an _____, your life will never be the same again.

🖵 THIRD VIEWING

Complete these notes as you watch the video. Use abbreviations and symbols.

1) hbs → from E. _____
   hbs in Afr. ↑↑ _____

2) 2 varieties of hb

Monticola	= gentle		_____ -colored	_____
Scutellata	_____	≠ calm		lots of honey

3) Stingless bees
   - In T.
   - 2 _____
   - v. _____ honey

4) Stanley = st b. _____ in Western _____.
   - keeps _____ species
   - inc. species _____ don't know

5) Crops need _____
   - ex: coffee and _____.

ORAL SUMMARY

Use your notes to create an oral summary of the video with your partner. As you work together, add details to your notes that your partner included but you had missed.

DISCUSSION

Discuss the following questions with a classmate or in a small group.

1. How are humans and honeybees similar?

2. What did the woman in the video learn? Why is she surprised? Did this information surprise you, too?

3. Why does Dino Martins ask the audience about chocolate and coffee?

4. Has this video changed your opinion of insects and entomologists? Why or why not?

Comparison and Contrast

Describing Similarities and Differences

A Great Dane and a little Chihuahua

CHAPTER 10

Asian and African Elephants

Similarities and Differences

TOPIC PREVIEW

Answer the following questions with a partner or your classmates.

1. Discuss the animals you see in the photo on this page. What do you know about these animals?

2. Have you ever seen a real elephant? Describe where and when you saw it. What impressed you most about the animal?

3. Talk about the similarities and differences between elephants (the largest animals that live on land) and whales (the largest animals that live in water).

A young elephant in Kaziranga National Park, India

VOCABULARY PREVIEW

CD 5, TR 1

A **Listen to the following sentences that contain information from the lecture. As you listen, write the word from the box that completes the sentence.**

enormous	fascinating	mammals	tamer	temperament
trained	trunk	tusks	wilder	

1. Today's topic is the largest land _____ on earth—elephants.

2. Elephants are _____ animals.

3. An elephant uses its _____ to put grasses, leaves, and water into its mouth.

4. Elephants can be _____ to do heavy work.

5. The Asian elephant sometimes does not have any _____ at all.

6. A big difference between the two types of elephants is their _____.

7. The Asian elephant is _____ than the African elephant.

8. The African elephant is much _____ than the Asian elephant.

9. There certainly are differences between the African and the Asian elephants, but they are both _____ animals.

B **Match the words to their definitions.**

_____ 1. mammal   a. the long nose of an elephant

_____ 2. enormous   b. to teach to do something

_____ 3. fascinating   c. easy for people to control and teach

_____ 4. tame   d. one of the two long teeth that an elephant has

_____ 5. temperament   e. very difficult for people to control

_____ 6. train   f. of very great or large size; huge

_____ 7. trunk   g. very interesting

_____ 8. tusk   h. nature; outlook; personality

_____ 9. wild   i. an animal that feeds its own milk to its babies

PREDICTIONS

Think about the questions in the Topic Preview on page 74 and the sentences you heard in the Vocabulary Preview. Write three questions that you think will be answered in the lecture. Share your questions with your classmates.

NOTETAKING PREPARATION

Making a Comparison Chart

As soon as a lecturer indicates that he or she is going to compare or contrast two things, a good notetaker will make a chart with two columns and put the name of the two things that are going to be compared at the top of the columns.

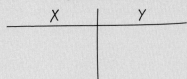

Listen for statements such as

There are two types of
*Today I am going to be talking about **X** and **Y***
*Today's lecture will compare and contrast **X** and **Y***

A well-planned lecture will compare each point in an organized way so that you can list each of the points opposite each other in the chart. When something is the same on both sides of the chart, you can save time by just putting a check (✓) in the second column.

🔊 CD 5, TR 2 **Ⓐ** **Listen to this short talk about two types of camels. As you listen, make a chart below and write in some details about each kind of camel.**

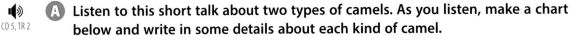

Discourse Cues for Comparison and Contrast   Listen for language that indicates that the lecturer is making a comparison. Key words and phrases to listen for are:

*Both **X** and **Y** . . .*
*One/another similarity is that **X** and **Y** . . .*
***X** and **Y** are alike in that . . .*

🔊 CD 5, TR 2 **Ⓑ** **Listen to part of the lecture. As you listen, count the number of times that the lecturer uses the word *both*. Circle your answer below.**

    a. 2   b. 3   c. 4   d. 5

FIRST LISTENING

CD 5, TR 3

Listen to the lecture on elephants. As you listen, put the following parts of the lecture in the order that you hear them. Number them 1 to 5.

_____ The continents elephants come from

_____ Elephants' temperaments

_____ Elephants' trunks

_____ Elephants' size

_____ Elephants' intelligence

SECOND LISTENING

CD 5, TR 4

Listen to information from the lecture. The speaker will talk slowly and carefully. You don't have to do anything as you listen. Just relax and listen.

THIRD LISTENING

Listen to the lecture in two parts. Follow the directions for each part. When you have finished, review your notes. Later, you will use them to summarize the lecture with a partner.

Part 1

CD 5, TR 5

You will hear the first part of the lecture again. Listen and complete the notes by adding the abbreviations and symbols from the box.

| ✓ | e.g. | gals | + | Afr. |

Asian E	_____ E
has trunk	✓
eats leaves + grass	
picks up obj _____ trees	
drinks 50 _____ H$_2$O per day	_____
intellgnt	✓
heavy work	
do tricks _____ entertain	

Part 2

CD 5, TR 5

As you listen to the second part of the lecture, take your own notes on a separate piece of paper.

ACCURACY CHECK

🔊 CD 5, TR 6

A You will hear four questions about the lecture. Listen to each question and write the letter of the best answer.

_____ 1. a. ear
     b. trunk
     c. tooth
     d. tusk

_____ 2. a. African elephants
     b. Asian elephants
     c. both Asian and African
     d. neither African nor Asian

_____ 3. a. 7,000 to 12,000 lbs.
     b. 8,000 to 10,000 lbs.
     c. 12,000 to 14,000 lbs.
     d. 18,000 to 20,000 lbs.

_____ 4. a. larger and lighter
     b. heavier and larger
     c. lighter and smaller
     d. smaller and heavier

🔊 CD 5, TR 6

B You will hear five statements about the lecture. Listen to each statement and decide if you heard the information in the lecture. Write *Y* for *yes* or *N* for *no*.

1. _____   2. _____   3. _____   4. _____   5. _____

ORAL SUMMARY

Use your notes to create an oral summary of the lecture with your partner. As you work together, add details to your notes that your partner included but you had missed.

DISCUSSION

Discuss the following questions with a classmate or in a small group.

1. Some people say the one animal that doesn't belong in a zoo is the elephant. Do you agree? Why? Do you think there are animals other than elephants that don't belong in zoos or circuses?

2. Compare two domestic animals (dog, cat, horse, etc.) and two wild animals (giraffe, bear, wolf, etc.). How are the two domestic animals similar and different? How are the two wild animals similar and different?

3. Some Asian elephants are working animals that are trained to do work such as lifting tree trunks for people. What animals do work in your country? What work do they do?

4. How are the kinds of pets sold in pet stores and those given away by animal rescue organizations such as the ASPCA similar or different?

TASK 1 The Hippo and the Rhino

 CD 5, TR 7

A Listen to the talk about the similarities and differences between the hippopotamus—the hippo—and the rhinoceros—the rhino. As you listen, complete the Venn diagram with the information below.

herbivores

have horns

loners

very big and heavy

endangered

eat at night

social animals

can be found in Asia

good swimmers

can be found in Africa

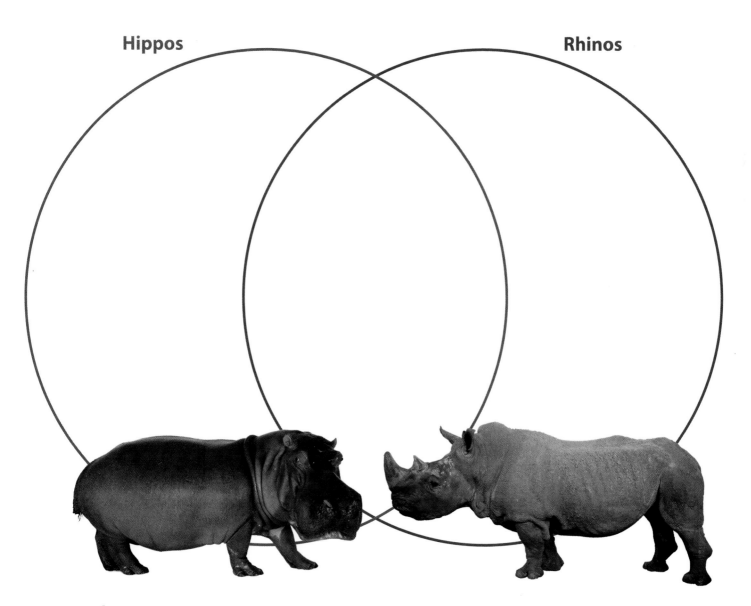

Hippos

Rhinos

B Compare your answers with a partner and make sentences that compare and contrast the two animals.

TASK 2 Two Brothers

CD 5, TR 8

A Listen for similarities and differences between two brothers, Charlie and David. As you listen, put a check (✓) in the correct box under each picture.

Charlie		David
☐	is married	☐
☐	has two children	☐
☐	has a girl and a boy	☐
☐	works in an office	☐
☐	works as a firefighter	☐
☐	likes jazz music	☐
☐	likes to play golf	☐
☐	is wealthy	☐

B Compare your answers with a partner.

Lincoln and Kennedy

Different Times, Similar Destinies

TOPIC PREVIEW

Answer the following questions with a partner or your classmates.

1. What do you know about Abraham Lincoln and John F. Kennedy? Talk about how you think the two men are similar and how they are different.

2. Do you know when Lincoln or Kennedy lived? What was happening in the United States at those times?

3. Both men met a sad end. Do you know what it was? Can you describe what happened to each man?

John F. Kennedy

Abraham Lincoln, Lincoln Memorial, Washington, DC

VOCABULARY PREVIEW

🔊
CD 5, TR 9

A Listen to the following sentences that contain information from the lecture. As you listen, write the word from the box that completes the sentence.

assassinated	career	coincidences	demonstrations	elected
fates	formal	rights	term	

1. I'll say a few words about Lincoln's and Kennedy's tragic _____.

2. Both Lincoln and Kennedy were _____ while in office.

3. In spite of his lack of _____ education, Lincoln became a well-known lawyer.

4. Books have been written about the strange _____ in the lives of the two men.

5. Lincoln began his political _____ in Congress.

6. Lincoln and Kennedy were _____ to Congress 100 years apart.

7. At the time Kennedy took office, African Americans were being denied their civil _____.

8. Unrest took the form of civil rights _____.

9. Neither president lived to complete his _____ in office.

B Match the words with their definitions.

_____ 1. assassinate   a. a set length of time for something, from start to finish

_____ 2. right   b. the things that happen to someone

_____ 3. coincidence   c. usual or official

_____ 4. career   d. a person's work

_____ 5. demonstration   e. something such as equality that all people have

_____ 6. elect   f. a public march or gathering when people show they
                             are for or against something

_____ 7. fate   g. to kill an important person, often for a political reason

_____ 8. formal   h. the surprising way two similar things happen

_____ 9. term   i. to choose someone by voting

PREDICTIONS

Think about the questions in the Topic Preview on page 81 and the sentences you heard in the Vocabulary Preview. Write three questions that you think will be answered in the lecture. Share your questions with your classmates.

NOTETAKING PREPARATION

Listening to the Lecture Overview

A good lecturer will very often begin the lecture by providing students with an overview of what will be talked about and in what order. Listen carefully to this overview and try to quickly write down and number the different sections of the lecture. As you listen to the rest of the lecture, use those numbers as the lecturer starts each new section.

The overview will very often contain language such as

First, I'm going to talk about . . .   *I'll also be talking about . . .*
Then I'll tell you . . .   *Finally, I'll end by . . .*

CD 5, TR 10

A **You will hear the beginnings of two lectures about U.S. presidents. Listen to the lecturer give an overview of lecture 1 and then of lecture 2. As you listen, write down and number the main sections of each lecture on the notepaper below.**

1.

2.

Discourse Cues for Comparison and Contrast

Listen for language cues that show that a lecturer is making or is going to make a contrast such as the following:

however   *one/another difference is*
whereas   *on the other hand*
while   *in contrast*

CD 5, TR 10

B **Listen to five sentences that contain information from the lecture. As you listen to each sentence, write the language cue you hear the lecturer use to make a contrast.**

1. _____

2. _____

3. _____

4. _____

5. _____

CD 5, TR 11

FIRST LISTENING

Listen to the lecture on Presidents Lincoln and Kennedy. As you listen, put the following parts of the lecture in the order that you hear them. Number them 1 to 5.

_____ Some coincidences in the lives of the two presidents

_____ The lecturer's personal memory of the death of President Kennedy

_____ Where the presidents were educated

_____ When the presidents were born

_____ The circumstances of the presidents' assassinations

CD 5, TR 12

SECOND LISTENING

Listen to information from the lecture. The speaker will talk slowly and carefully. You don't have to do anything as you listen. Just relax and listen.

THIRD LISTENING

Listen to the lecture in two parts. Follow the directions for each part. When you have finished, review your notes. Later, you will use them to summarize the lecture with a partner.

CD 5, TR 13

Part 1

You will hear the first part of the lecture again. Listen and complete the notes by adding the abbreviations and symbols from the box.

fam	ed	c	Polit.	b.

Overview

1. Diffs   2. Fam. lives   3. _____ lives   4. Trag. fates

Kennedy	Lincoln
20 _____	19c
b. 1917	_____ 1809
rich _____	not rich
exp. schools + Harvard	1 yr of form ed
	self _____ man

CD 5, TR 13

Part 2

As you listen to the second part of the lecture, take your own notes on a separate piece of paper.

ACCURACY CHECK

CD 5, TR 14

You will hear 10 questions about the lecture. Write a short answer to each question. Use your notes.

1. _____
2. _____
3. _____
4. _____
5. _____
6. _____
7. _____
8. _____
9. _____
10. _____

ORAL SUMMARY

Use your notes to create an oral summary of the lecture with your partner. As you work together, add details to your notes that your partner included but you had missed.

DISCUSSION

Discuss the following questions with a classmate or in a small group.

1. Read the quotations below. What do they mean to you?

   A house divided against itself can not stand. —Abraham Lincoln

   Ask not what your country can do for you, ask what you can do for your country. —John F. Kennedy

2. There have been conflicting theories about the assassination of John F. Kennedy: the "lone assassin" theory and the "conspiracy" theory. Do you know what these theories are? Explain what you think they mean.

3. What do the following statements say about how people "rally around," or support, their leaders during times of crisis? Explain.

   Kennedy's highest approval rating as president came right after the disastrous invasion of Cuba at the Bay of Pigs.

   President George H. W. Bush experienced his highest levels of popular support at the time of the Gulf War.

TASK 1 Two First Ladies

Mrs. Jacqueline Bouvier Kennedy,
wife of President John F. Kennedy

Mrs. Mary Todd Lincoln,
wife of President Abraham Lincoln

CD 5, TR 15

Listen to five similarities between the wives of President Lincoln and President Kennedy. You will hear each similarity twice. Write below exactly what you hear.

1. _____

2. _____

3. _____

4. _____

5. _____

TASK 2 Two Vice Presidents

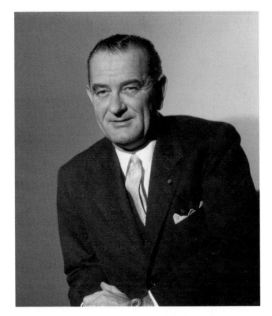

Vice President Lyndon Johnson,
President Kennedy's vice president

Vice President Andrew Johnson,
President Lincoln's vice president

CD 5, TR 16

A **Listen to these interesting differences and similarities between Kennedy's vice president, Lyndon Johnson, and Lincoln's vice president, Andrew Johnson. Circle** *similarity* **if you hear a similarity or** *difference* **if you hear difference.**

1. SIMILARITY   DIFFERENCE   5. SIMILARITY   DIFFERENCE

2. SIMILARITY   DIFFERENCE   6. SIMILARITY   DIFFERENCE

3. SIMILARITY   DIFFERENCE   7. SIMILARITY   DIFFERENCE

4. SIMILARITY   DIFFERENCE

CD 5, TR 16

B **Listen again to the statements about the two vice presidents. Take notes about each similarity or difference.**

1. _____

2. _____

3. _____

4. _____

5. _____

6. _____

7. _____

C **Compare your notes with a partner and check to see if you circled the correct word,** *similarity* **or** *difference,* **in A above.**

CHAPTER 12

The *Titanic* and the *Costa Concordia*

Tragedies at Sea

TOPIC PREVIEW

Answer the following questions with a partner or a classmate.

1. Describe the picture on this page. What do you think is happening?

2. Have you ever seen a movie or a video about the sinking of a ship? What was the name of the movie? What was the story like? What did you like or dislike about the movie?

3. What do you expect to find on the ship if you decide to take a vacation cruise?

The Italian cruise ship *Costa Concordia*, on the rocks, January 2012

VOCABULARY PREVIEW

CD 6, TR 1

A Listen to the following sentences that contain information from the lecture. As you listen, write the word or phrase from the box that completes the sentence.

courage	cowardice	disasters	iceberg	lifeboats
partial	set sail	shelf	sink	

1. On the morning of April 10, 1912, the *Titanic* _____ from England.

2. Reports of the sinking—or the _____ sinking—of the *Costa Concordia* filled the newspapers, television, and the Internet for days.

3. As each ship was sinking, there were acts of _____.

4. Some men on the *Titanic* gave up their seats in the _____ to women and children.

5. So, on the *Costa Concordia*, there were also acts of courage and acts of _____.

6. I'd like to point out some of the big differences between these two ship _____.

7. Another difference was what caused these ships to _____.

8. The *Titanic* struck an _____.

9. The *Costa Concordia* struck a _____ of rocks near an island.

B Match the words to their definitions.

_____ 1. courage   a. not complete or not entirely

_____ 2. iceberg   b. fear and a lack of ability to help in a dangerous situation

_____ 3. set sail

_____ 4. lifeboat   c. an event that causes a lot of damage and injury

_____ 5. cowardice   d. the ability to overcome fear when there is danger

_____ 6. sink   e. a long, flat area of rock under the water

_____ 7. partial   f. to begin a trip on a boat or ship

_____ 8. shelf   g. a large piece of ice that is floating in the ocean

_____ 9. disaster   h. to fall under water

     i. a boat used to rescue people from ships in trouble

PREDICTIONS

Think about the questions in the Topic Preview on page 88 and the sentences you heard in the Vocabulary Preview. Write three questions that you think will be answered in the lecture. Share your questions with your classmates.

NOTETAKING PREPARATION

Making Your Notes Complete

It is very difficult to take complete notes. Sometimes you can't hear or you miss some information. Sometimes you don't understand what the lecturer just said. And sometimes your mind wanders and you simply stop listening for a few seconds.

When these things happen, do the following:

- Make sure that you leave a space in your notes so that you can come back later and fill in missing information. Put a question mark in or next to the space.

- Arrange to meet after class with some classmates. Ask everyone to share their notes so that as a group you can fill in each other's missing information.

- Ask the lecturer for the information that you missed when the lecture is finished.

CD 6, TR 2

A The notes to the right are incomplete. Listen to a conversation between the notetaker, Alicia, and a classmate, Carlos, and fill in the notes with the missing information that Carlos provides.

> 1) On C.C. acts of courage and cow   ?
> - ev man for himself
> - capt of C.C. left ship   ?
>
> ?
>
> - many think capt – leave ship last
> - capt of T. died
> - capt of C.C.   ?

Discourse Cues for Comparison and Contrast   When a lecturer is comparing and contrasting two things, listen for discourse cues that tell you if the lecturer is expressing a similarity or a difference.

CD 6, TR 2

B Listen to sentences that contain information from the lecture. As you listen, write the missing words from each sentence in the blanks.

1. _____ the *Titanic* and the *Concordia* were enormous luxury ships.

2. The *Titanic* struck an iceberg, _____ the *Costa Concordia* struck rocks.

3. Another _____ is that as each ship was sinking there were acts of great courage.

4. There were not enough lifeboats on the *Titanic*. _____
   _____, there were plenty of lifeboats on the *Costa Concordia*.

5. People lost their lives on the *Concordia*; _____, there was much greater loss of life on the *Titanic*.

FIRST LISTENING

CD 6, TR 3

Listen to the lecture on the sinking of two ships. As you listen, put the following parts of the lecture in the order that you hear them. Number them 1 to 5.

_____ Acts of courage and cowardice aboard the two ships

_____ The size of the ships

_____ The number of people who died and survived

_____ The general safety of traveling

_____ Where and why the ships went down

SECOND LISTENING

CD 6, TR 4

Listen to information from the lecture. The speaker will talk slowly and carefully. You don't have to do anything as you listen. Just relax and listen.

THIRD LISTENING

Listen to the lecture in two parts. Follow the directions for each part. When you have finished, review your notes. Later, you will use them to summarize the lecture with a partner.

Part 1

CD 6, TR 5

You will hear the first part of the lecture again. Listen and complete the notes by adding the abbreviations and symbols from the box.

lux	enorm	1st	+	3)

Titanic sail Apr 10, 1912   Costa Concordia — ? 2012

Similarities

1) Both _____

    T. — 882 ft + 9 decks

    C.C. — 951 ft _____ 13 decks

2) Both _____ ships

    Pools, restaurants etc.

    _____ On both ships acts of courag and coward

    On T. — men let women + child. _____

    But . . . one man dressed as woman

Part 2

CD 6, TR 5

As you listen to the second part of the lecture, take your own notes on a separate piece of paper.

ACCURACY CHECK

CD 6, TR 6

A You will hear eight questions about the lecture. Listen to each question and write the letter of the best answer.

_____ 1. a. January 13, 1910
b. January 13, 2012
c. April 10, 1912
d. April 10, 2012

_____ 2. a. England
b. Italy
c. the United States
d. none of the above

_____ 3. a. Both were over 880 feet long.
b. Both were luxury liners.
c. Both sank in deep water.
d. Both sailed to Italy.

_____ 4. a. *Titanic* sank in shallow water.
b. *Titanic* was the taller ship.
c. *Costa Concordia* hit rocks.
d. *Costa Concordia* was small.

_____ 5. a. the *Titanic*
b. the *Costa Concordia*
c. both a and b
d. none of the above

_____ 6. a. 25
b. 32
c. 700
d. 1,500

_____ 7. a. It struck an iceberg.
b. It struck a shelf of rocks.
c. It ran into another ship.
d. It had enough lifeboats.

_____ 8. a. Accidents can happen.
b. Disaster is possible.
c. Most ships arrive safely.
d. all of the above

B You will hear six statements about the lecture. Listen to each statement and decide if it mentions a similarity or a difference. Write *S* for *similarity* or *D* for *difference*.

1. _____   2. _____   3. _____   4. _____   5. _____   6. _____

ORAL SUMMARY

Use your notes to create an oral summary of the lecture with your partner. As you work together, add details to your notes that your partner included but you had missed.

DISCUSSION

Discuss the following questions with a classmate or in a small group.

1. Compare how you travel within your country to how you travel between countries. Do you travel by plane, train, car, ship, or another way? Why?

2. What do you think you would enjoy doing if you went on a cruise? What would you not like to do on a cruise? Explain.

3. Compare and contrast two transportation disasters that happened in your country or somewhere else. What happened? What was the result of these tragedies?

TASK 1 The Hindenburg Disaster

CD 6, TR 7

Listen to sentences comparing the 1937 _Hindenburg_ disaster with the 1912 _Titanic_ disaster. As you listen, write missing words in the blanks to complete the sentences.

1. The _Hindenburg_ and the _Titanic_ were both _____ passenger ships. The _____ was that one of them was an airship and the other was an _____ liner.

2. _____ vessels created a lot of excitement among the general _____. They both represented the beginning of a new era of luxury _____.

3. The _Titanic_ sank on its maiden voyage after hitting an iceberg. The _Hindenburg_, on the other _____, caught fire and crashed on its _____ voyage.

4. Like the _Titanic_, there were _____ from the _Hindenburg_ crash. Of the 97 people on board the _Hindenburg_, 35 people died and _____ survived.

5. No news crews _____ the sinking of the _Titanic_. However, the crash of the _Hindenburg_ was _____. One reporter, Herbert Morrison, gave a breathless account that millions listened to on the _____.

TASK 2 Easily Confused Words

CD 6, TR 8

Listen to descriptions of some easily confused words. Write the word you hear next to its correct description.

1. _____ : many people like you

   _____ : many people know about you

2. _____ : very well-known

   _____ : well-known because of doing something bad

3. _____ : unpopular, and feeling bad about it

   _____ : not with other people

4. _____ : not many

   _____ : describing a small but positive number

Free Soloing with Alex Honnold

TOPIC PREVIEW

Work with a partner to make a list or draw pictures in the box below. Draw or list the different pieces of equipment mountain climbers use to keep them safe when they climb.

VOCABULARY PREVIEW

A Read the definitions of these key words and phrases that you will hear during the video.

gear special equipment used to do a particular activity or sport

at the top of [this] game at the very highest level of ability

unbelievably gifted with an amazing, incredible natural talent

revolves around turns in a circle about a central point that is the focus

memorable moments times that are so enjoyable or important in your life that you expect you will always remember them

switched changed

well within his ability something that he could easily do

awesome amazing, extraordinary, fantastic, wonderful

B Work with a partner and discuss answers to the following questions.

1. Is there anything that is **well within your ability** to do but not easy for other people that you know?

2. Does your life **revolve around** a particular person, place, or activity?

3. In what areas can some people be **unbelievably gifted**?

4. What special **gear** do you need to do an activity that you enjoy doing?

5. Describe a time when you decided to stop doing something and to **switch** and do something different.

6. At what age do you think you were **at the top of your game**?

7. What experiences have you had that you would describe as "**awesome**" or "**memorable moments**"?

VIEWING

🖥 FIRST VIEWING

Watch the video, and then compare your first impressions with a partner. Talk about what you remember, what surprised you, and what interested you.

🖥 SECOND VIEWING

Watch the video again. Listen for the missing words and write them in the blanks.

1. Free soloing has to be the ultimate in free _____.

2. The reason it's probably the ultimate is because one _____ move, you fall, you die.

3. Yeah, I would say that Yosemite probably is the _____ of my climbing.

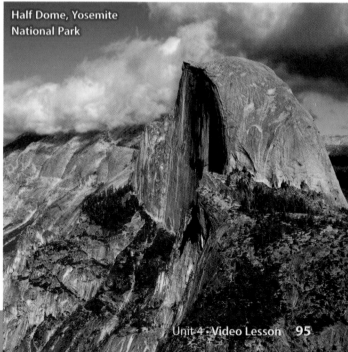

Half Dome, Yosemite National Park

4. For most people on this planet who are serious climbers, doing Half Dome in a day or two is considered _____. Alex did it in three hours, without a _____.

5. I've sort of embraced the whole _____, you know, embraced the unpleasant parts, too.

Complete these notes as you watch the video. Write only important words, not full sentences, and abbreviate common words.

1) Free soloing
   FS = ultim _____
   FS = w/o _____, _____, pwr of _____
      w/ _____, _____, chalk _____
      _____ → death

2) Yosemite – ctr of climbing
   • _____
   • _____
   • Half Dome – _____

3) Tired/stalled out
   • _____
   • _____

4) Last season
   • _____
   • _____
   • Awesome!

AFTER VIEWING

ORAL SUMMARY

Use your notes to create an oral summary of the video with your partner. As you work together, add details to your notes that your partner included but you had missed.

DISCUSSION

Discuss the following questions with a classmate or in a small group.

1. Why does the narrator, Jenkins, say that Alex Honnold is "like Michael Jordan"?

2. How is free soloing different from how most climbers climb?

3. What is something you have done to "stretch your limits," that is, something that is physically difficult and challenging for you?

Cause and Effect

Describing the Reason Things Happen

Polar bear surrounded by melting Arctic pack ice

CHAPTER 13

Dinosaurs

Why They Disappeared

TOPIC PREVIEW

Answer the following questions with a partner or your classmates.

1. Only the bones of the dinosaurs can be seen today, mainly in museums. Have you ever seen the bones of a dinosaur? Describe when and where you saw them. If you haven't seen any, would you like to see dinosaur bones? Why?

2. Describe what a *Tyrannosaurus rex* or another type of dinosaur probably looked like. When did this dinosaur live on earth, how large was it, and what was its food?

3. What is climate change? Do we feel the influence of climate change today? Why or why not?

Dinosaur skeletons on display at the National Museum of Natural History, Leiden, The Netherlands

VOCABULARY PREVIEW

CD 6, TR 9

A **Listen to the following sentences that contain information from the lecture. As you listen, write the word or phrase from the box that completes the sentence.**

| asteroid | blocked out | died out | debate | element |
| extinct | gradual | shortage | speculate | |

1. Scientists suggest several theories for why dinosaurs became _____.

2. Perhaps one day we will know for certain why dinosaurs such as the *Tyrannosaurus rex* _____.

3. We continue to _____ and to search for why dinosaurs disappeared.

4. The change in climate caused a severe _____ of food.

5. Many scientists believe that _____ climate change best explains why the dinosaurs disappeared.

6. The second theory suggests that a huge _____ hit the earth 65 million years ago when the dinosaurs still walked the earth.

7. The enormous dust cloud covered the whole earth and _____ the sun for months and months.

8. Iridium is an _____ that is not common on earth.

9. Today scientists continue to _____ these two theories and others, too.

B **Match the words to their definitions.**

_____ 1. die out   a. to make guesses about something

_____ 2. speculate   b. not existing any longer

_____ 3. gradual   c. to slowly disappear over time and stop existing

_____ 4. element   d. to talk about the different ideas about something

_____ 5. debate   e. a rock moving through outer space

_____ 6. extinct   f. to prevent light or sound from reaching somewhere

_____ 7. asteroid   g. a situation where there is too little of something

_____ 8. block out   h. little by little; happening very, very slowly

_____ 9. shortage   i. a substance that cannot be broken down into smaller parts

PREDICTIONS

Think about the questions in the Topic Preview on page 98 and the sentences you heard in the Vocabulary Preview. Write three questions that you think will be answered in the lecture. Share your questions with your classmates.

NOTETAKING PREPARATION

Using Arrows for Cause and Effect

You learned in Chapter 2 that arrows are very useful symbols. When a lecturer describes the causes and effect of events, use arrows in your notes to show what is the cause and what is the effect by the direction the arrow points. The arrow should always point to the effect.

You hear	You write
X causes Y	$X \rightarrow Y$
X is the result of Y	$X \leftarrow Y$

A Listen to the following causes and effects described in the lecture. Use either → or ← to complete the notes below.

CD 6, TR 10

1. Dinos extinct _____ plnt clim change

2. Clim cooler _____ dinos disapp

3. Ast hit earth _____ v. big cloud dust

4. Food vanish _____ dinos too

5. Perhps find dinos die _____ disease

Discourse Cues for Causal Analysis   Listen for language cues that indicate that the lecturer is describing causes and effects.

Verbs	Nouns	Transitions	Conjunctions
cause	cause	therefore	because (of)
result in/from	result	as a result (of)	since
lead to	reason	for this reason	so

B Listen to the sentences in **A** again. As you listen, write the complete sentences below.

CD 6, TR 10

1. Dinosaurs became extinct _____.

2. The climate of the world became cooler. _____.

3. When the asteroid hit the earth, _____.

4. Their food vanished, _____.

5. Perhaps they'll find out that dinosaurs died out _____.

🔊 FIRST LISTENING
CD 6, TR 11

Listen to the lecture about dinosaurs. As you listen, put the following parts of the lecture in the order that you hear them. Number them 1 to 5.

_____ The asteroid impact theory

_____ Possible other theories

_____ The climate change theory

_____ Two different theories that some scientists believe today

_____ Iridium in earth as evidence of asteroid theory

🔊 SECOND LISTENING
CD 6, TR 12

Listen to information from the lecture. The speaker will talk slowly and carefully. You don't have to do anything as you listen. Just relax and listen.

THIRD LISTENING

Listen to the lecture in two parts. Follow the directions for each part. When you have finished, review your notes. Later, you will use them to summarize the lecture with a partner.

🔊 Part 1
CD 6, TR 13

You will hear the first part of the lecture again. Listen and complete the notes by adding the abbreviations and symbols from the box.

| ext | Qs | → | dinos | 3) |

Why Dinos Disappear?
1) 2 _____ • wh happened to dinos?
                • why _____ disapp?
2) Not sure — 2 theories
   1. clim. change theory
   2. asteroid theory
   _____ Climate theory
      over millions yrs — climate cooler
      → plants died → short of food _____
      no food for dinos → become _____

🔊 Part 2
CD 6, TR 13

As you listen to the second part of the lecture, take your own notes on a separate piece of paper.

ACCURACY CHECK

CD 6, TR 14

A You will hear five questions about the lecture. Write a short answer to each question. Use your notes.

1. _____

2. _____

3. _____

4. _____

5. _____

CD 6, TR 14

B You will hear five statements about the lecture. Listen to each statement and write *T* for *true* or *F* for *false*.

1. _____   2. _____   3. _____   4. _____   5. _____

ORAL SUMMARY

Use your notes to create an oral summary of the lecture with your partner. As you work together, add details to your notes that your partner included but you had missed.

DISCUSSION

Discuss the following questions with a classmate or in a small group.

1. Which of the two theories, the asteroid impact theory or the gradual climate-change theory, do you think best explains the disappearance of the dinosaurs?

2. What do you suggest as another theory for why the dinosaurs disappeared? Use your imagination to come up with some possible causes.

3. What are the names of some dinosaurs you are familiar with? Draw a picture of a dinosaur as you picture it in your mind. Describe what it is doing in your picture.

4. Some scientists think today's birds and perhaps some lizards, such as the Komodo dragon, are descendants of the dinosaurs of the past. Do you agree? Why or why not?

TASK 1 What's the Reason?

CD 6, TR 15

A Listen to the situations. As you listen, decide if a, b, c, or d is the cause. Circle your answer.

1. a. You are sitting too close to it.
   b. The set isn't plugged in.
   c. You forgot to pay your telephone bill.
   d. You forgot to pay your electricity bill.

2. a. The park is near her house.
   b. Her best friend is going to be there.
   c. The weather is warm and sunny.
   d. She has to study for an exam.

3. a. He often gave too much money to customers by mistake.
   b. He found a new job immediately.
   c. He was sometimes rude to the customers.
   d. He doesn't have enough money to pay his bills.

4. a. His grandmother was French.
   b. He liked living in Paris.
   c. He went to Paris to get a job.
   d. His parents lived there in the 1970s.

5. a. The teacher didn't like Antonia.
   b. The examination was very easy.
   c. The examination was too difficult for the class.
   d. Antonia didn't understand the directions for the test.

6. a. Your doctor is out of town.
   b. You can't find your phone.
   c. The doctor's office is very busy when you call.
   d. The doctor's phone is out of order.

7. a. Tony was very unlucky.
   b. It's very expensive to fly to Monte Carlo.
   c. Tony doesn't have enough money to get home.
   d. Tony doesn't like to lose money when he gambles.

8. a. He is a soccer player.
   b. He has just finished playing tennis.
   c. His wife is getting ready to play tennis.
   d. He is going to play volleyball.

B Compare your answers with a partner.

TASK 2 You Write the Ending

CD 6, TR 16

A **Listen to five unfinished stories. Take notes about what happens.**

1. It's a cold and snowy night.

2. It's the second half of a championship soccer game.

3. A fisherman is walking by the side of the river.

4. You and your friend are sitting in the movie theater watching a movie.

5. A man is crossing a street in New York.

B **Look at your notes and create an ending for each story. Tell your ending to the stories to a classmate.**

CHAPTER 14

The U.S. Civil War

Why It Happened

TOPIC PREVIEW

Answer the following questions with a partner or your classmates.

1. What is a civil war? What kinds of situations can cause a civil war to happen? Name a civil war that happened in the past and briefly talk about the causes and results of this civil war.

2. What do you know about the U.S. Civil War? What caused this war? What role did slavery play in the war?

3. What do you know about Abraham Lincoln and his role in the U.S. Civil War?

Painting showing the Battle of Gettysburg, 1863

VOCABULARY PREVIEW

🔊
CD 7, TR 1

A Listen to the following sentences that contain information from the lecture. As you listen, write the word or phrase from the box that completes the sentence.

| descendant | devastation | dominate | foundation | plantations |
| secede | tension | vital | way of life | |

1. I'm a _____ of a soldier who fought for the Union—that is, the North—in the Civil War.

2. There were a number of reasons for _____ between the North and the South.

3. Slavery was, in fact, the _____ of the economy in the South.

4. In the South there were large _____ that grew cotton and tobacco.

5. Many Southerners feared that the North would _____ the country.

6. When Abraham Lincoln became President of the United States, the South decided it was time to _____ from the Union.

7. The people of the South were afraid that their _____ was in danger.

8. The Civil War led to the _____ of the South.

9. The South today is a _____ part of these United States.

B Match the words to their definitions.

_____ 1. tension		a. very important; necessary
_____ 2. devastation		b. a child or relative of someone who lived in the past
_____ 3. foundation		c. to leave a group, organization, or country
_____ 4. dominate		d. a large farm where a particular crop is grown to be sold
_____ 5. secede		e. an anxious feeling when people don't trust each other
_____ 6. way of life		f. the usual way a person or a group of people lives
_____ 7. descendant		g. serious damage caused to a people, area, or country
_____ 8. vital		h. the part on which other parts rest or depend for support
_____ 9. plantation		i. to control or rule by strength or power

PREDICTIONS

Think about the questions in the Topic Preview on page 105 and the sentences you heard in the Vocabulary Preview. Write three questions that you think will be answered in the lecture. Share your questions with your classmates.

NOTETAKING PREPARATION

When Not to Take Notes

It's not always necessary to take notes on everything a lecturer says. For example, the lecturer may tell a personal story or give information that is not directly related to the main points of the lecture. When the lecturer starts to do that, you don't need to take notes.

A **Listen to parts of the lecture on the causes of the U.S. Civil War. Decide if you need to take notes on those parts or don't need to take notes. Circle your answers, a or b.**

1. a. need to take notes   b. don't need to take notes

2. a. need to take notes   b. don't need to take notes

3. a. need to take notes   b. don't need to take notes

4. a. need to take notes   b. don't need to take notes

5. a. need to take notes   b. don't need to take notes

6. a. need to take notes   b. don't need to take notes

Discourse Cues for Causal Analysis   In academic classes, lectures don't just describe what happened and when. A good lecturer will analyze events and help students think about why things happened. As the lecturer discusses causes, he or she will use certain discourse cues. Make sure that you learn these and can recognize when the lecturer has moved from describing to analyzing.

For a list of discourse cues see page 100.

B **Listen to sentences that contain information from the lecture. As you listen to each sentence, write the words and phrases that the lecturer uses to discuss cause and effect.**

1. _____

2. _____

3. _____

4. _____

5. _____

6. _____

LISTENING

FIRST LISTENING

CD 7, TR 3

Listen to the lecture on the U.S. Civil War. As you listen, put the following parts of the lecture in the order that you hear them. Number them 1 to 5.

_____ The attitude of Northerners and Southerners to slavery

_____ The strong economy of the northern states

_____ Lincoln's election as a cause of the civil war

_____ Statistics about how many people died during the U.S. Civil War

_____ The importance of slavery to southern agriculture

SECOND LISTENING

CD 7, TR 4

Listen to information from the lecture. The speaker will talk slowly and carefully. You don't have to do anything as you listen. Just relax and listen.

THIRD LISTENING

Listen to the lecture in two parts. Follow the directions for each part. When you have finished, review your notes. Later, you will use them to summarize the lecture with a partner.

CD 7, TR 5

Part 1

You will hear the first part of the lecture again. Listen and complete the notes by adding the abbreviations and symbols from the box.

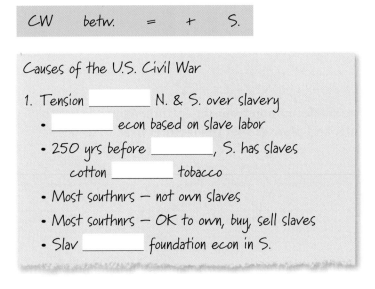

CW   betw.   =   +   S.

Causes of the U.S. Civil War

1. Tension _____ N. & S. over slavery
   - _____ econ based on slave labor
   - 250 yrs before _____, S. has slaves
     cotton _____ tobacco
   - Most southnrs — not own slaves
   - Most southnrs — OK to own, buy, sell slaves
   - Slav _____ foundation econ in S.

Part 2

CD 7, TR 5

As you listen to the second part of the lecture, take your own notes on a separate piece of paper.

ACCURACY CHECK

CD 7, TR 6

A You will hear four questions about the lecture. Write a short answer to each question. Use your notes.

1. _____

2. _____

3. _____

4. _____

CD 7, TR 6

B You will hear two sentences. One sentence mentions a cause and the other sentence gives the effect. You will be asked for either the *cause* or the *effect*. Write your answers below.

1. _____

2. _____

3. _____

4. _____

5. _____

ORAL SUMMARY

Use your notes to create an oral summary of the lecture with your partner. As you work together, add details to your notes that your partner included but you had missed.

DISCUSSION

Discuss the following questions with a classmate or in a small group.

1. Almost 200 movies have been made about the U.S. Civil War such as *Gone with the Wind* and *Gettysburg*. Can you name any others? Have you seen one? Or have you seen a movie about another civil war? How well did the movie show the causes and effects of the war?

2. You heard in the lecture that the U.S. Civil War is called other names such as the War between the States, the War of Rebellion, the War of Northern Aggression. Why do you think there are these different names and who do you think used them?

3. Discuss the causes and effects of one of the following: (1) an illness; (2) a trip to another country; (3) running a marathon; (4) winning an Olympic gold medal.

TASK 1 The Revolutionary War

CD 7, TR 7

Listen to sentences about the American Revolution. As you listen, complete the sentences by writing the missing words in the blanks.

1. The American Revolution started _____ the colonists wanted to have some form of _____ .

2. The British were at a disadvantage during the war on _____ of the _____ that they were fighting a war far from their _____ country.

3. _____ the colonists had fewer weapons and _____ than the British, at times the colonists used some guerilla warfare _____ .

4. One _____ that the colonists won the war was _____ the French entered the war on their _____ .

TASK 2 Guessing Causes

CD 7, TR 8

Listen to each of the following situations. After you listen to each situation, quickly write down a possible cause or causes for the event you hear described.

1. Possible causes:

   _____

   _____

   _____

   _____

   _____

   _____

2. Possible causes:

   _____

   _____

   _____

   _____

   _____

   _____

3. Possible causes:

_____

_____

_____

_____

_____

_____

4. Possible causes:

_____

_____

_____

_____

_____

_____

5. Possible causes:

_____

_____

_____

_____

_____

_____

6. Possible causes:

_____

_____

_____

_____

_____

_____

CHAPTER 15

Endangered Species

Why Are They Endangered?

TOPIC PREVIEW

Answer the following questions with a partner or your classmates.

1. Think of an animal or plant species that is in danger of disappearing from the earth. Why is the animal or plant endangered?

2. What kinds of things do humans do that endanger species like the African elephant or rhinoceros? How do people help protect endangered species such as these animals?

3. How does air and water pollution endanger some species of fish, birds, and animals?

An endangered tortoise risks its life crossing the road in Wiggins, Mississippi.

VOCABULARY PREVIEW

CD 7, TR 9

A Listen to the following sentences that contain information from the lecture. As you listen, write the word or phrase from the box that completes the sentence.

adapted	clear	dams	horns
introduced	related to	souvenirs	wildlife

1. Most animals and plants are _____ to live in a very specific environment.

2. Farmers _____ land to grow crops on.

3. We build _____ across rivers to produce electricity.

4. Closely _____ the destruction of habitats is the pollution of the environment.

5. Another major reason so many species are endangered is the illegal trade in _____.

6. Elephant tusks are used to make _____ to sell to tourists.

7. Rhinoceroses, or rhinos, are killed for their _____.

8. Some native species face competition from _____ species.

B Match the words to their definitions.

_____ 1. introduce

_____ 2. souvenir

_____ 3. wildlife

_____ 4. horn

_____ 5. clear

_____ 6. related to

_____ 7. dam

_____ 8. adapt

a. to put an animal or plant in a new region and environment

b. to become used to and depend on particular conditions

c. wild animals, birds, fish, etc., in their natural environment

d. a wall built to hold back water and make a lake

e. a hard pointed part growing from the head of some animals

f. something you buy or keep to remember a place you visited

g. to remove existing trees and other plants from an area of land

h. connected with another thing

PREDICTIONS

Think about the questions in the Topic Preview on page 112 and the sentences you heard in the Vocabulary Preview. Write three questions that you think will be answered in the lecture. Share your questions with your classmates.

NOTETAKING PREPARATION

Listening for a Review of the Lecture

Lecturers often repeat the main points of their lecture in their concluding remarks. Pay careful attention to this review at the end of a lecture and see if you have included the main points in your notes. If you find you have missed some important point, you can check after the lecture with your classmates or the lecturer to make your notes complete.

Listen for language such as the following to know that a review of the lecture is coming:

So, to review . . .
So, to sum up . . .
So, let me finish by going over the main points of today's lecture again.
I'd like to finish by reviewing the main points of my lecture . . .

CD 7, TR 10

A **As you hear each statement, decide what the lecturer is next going to do: a, b, c, or d. Circle your choice.**

| a. preview the whole lecture | c. review the whole lecture |
| b. preview a main point in the lecture | d. review a main point in the lecture |

1. a. b. c. d.   4. a. b. c. d.

2. a. b. c. d.   5. a. b. c. d.

3. a. b. c. d.   6. a. b. c. d.

Discourse Cues for Causal Analysis   Listen for the discourse cues that signal that a lecturer is discussing causes and effects. For a list of discourse cues for cause and effect, see page 100.

CD 7, TR 10

B **Listen to sentences that contain information from the lecture. As you listen, write the missing words in the blanks to complete each sentence.**

1. Most animals have disappeared from this planet _____ of natural _____ such as climate change.

2. Burning coal and oil can _____ acid rain, which results _____ a great deal of harm to an animal's habitat.

3. Competition for their habitat is a major _____ that animals are endangered. This is primarily a direct _____ of human activity.

4. Humans are also part of the natural world. _____, we need to protect plants and animals in order to protect our own future as a species.

FIRST LISTENING

CD 7, TR 11

Listen to the lecture on endangered species. As you listen, put the following parts of the lecture in the order that you hear them. Number them 1 to 5.

_____ Effects of rabbits introduced to Australia and brown tree snakes to Guam

_____ Different ways in which humans have destroyed animal habitats

_____ Reasons some animals are illegally hunted

_____ Human beings as a possible endangered species

_____ The effects of acid rain

SECOND LISTENING

CD 7, TR 12

Listen to information from the lecture. The speaker will talk slowly and carefully. You don't have to do anything as you listen. Just relax and listen.

THIRD LISTENING

Listen to the lecture in two parts. Follow the directions for each part. When you have finished, review your notes. Later, you will use them to summarize the lecture with a partner.

CD 7, TR 13

Part 1

You will hear the first part of the lecture again. Listen and complete the notes by adding the abbreviations and symbols from the box.

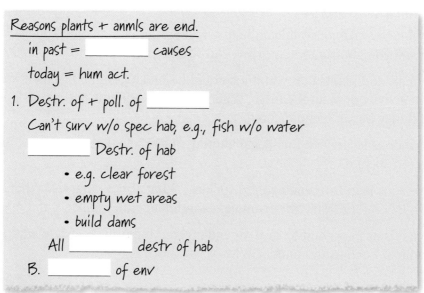

| hab | Poll. | nat | → | A. |

> Reasons plants + anmls are end.
>   in past = _____ causes
>   today = hum act.
> 1. Destr. of + poll. of _____
>   Can't surv w/o spec hab, e.g., fish w/o water
>   _____ Destr. of hab
>   • e.g. clear forest
>   • empty wet areas
>   • build dams
>   All _____ destr of hab
>   B. _____ of env

CD 7, TR 13

Part 2

As you listen to the second part of the lecture, take your own notes on a separate piece of paper.

CD 7, TR 14

ACCURACY CHECK

You will hear 10 questions about the lecture. Write a short answer to each question. Use your notes.

1. _____
2. _____
3. _____
4. _____
5. _____
6. _____
7. _____
8. _____
9. _____
10. _____

ORAL SUMMARY

Use your notes to create an oral summary of the lecture with your partner. As you work together, add details to your notes that your partner included but you had missed.

DISCUSSION

Discuss the following questions with a classmate or in a small group.

1. What actions can you take personally to help safeguard an endangered species? Which one would you choose to help? How can you help?

2. Name two animals and plants that you think could be endangered 50 years from now by human activity or natural causes. Where do these animals and plants live and why would they become endangered?

3. What should be done to prevent the illegal hunting of elephants, rhinos, tigers, and other endangered species?

4. Do you believe zoos help save endangered species? What about circuses? What about research laboratories that, for example, experiment with monkeys and mice?

5. Do you believe it is as important to save an endangered butterfly as it is to save an endangered animal, such as the panda? Why or why not?

TASK 1 Endangered Species

CD 7, TR 15

A **Listen to a short talk about endangered species. As you listen, fill in the missing information in the chart below.**

Animal	Habitat	Reasons Endangered
Giant panda	China	1. Habitat destruction 2.
Blue whale		1. Killed for its meat 2.
California condor	Southern California, Arizona	1. 2. Killed to protect domestic animals
Snow leopard		1. Killed for fur 2.

CD 7, TR 15

B **Listen to the questions. Write a short answer to each question you hear.**

1. _____
2. _____
3. _____
4. _____

TASK 2 Types of Pollution

CD 7, TR 16

Listen to descriptions of the causes of five different types of pollution. As you listen, write the number of the description next to the type of pollution it causes.

_____ Noise pollution

_____ Light pollution

_____ Land pollution

_____ Air pollution

_____ Water pollution

The Surma People

BEFORE VIEWING

TOPIC PREVIEW

Look at the photo and answer the following questions with a partner.

1. Where do you think the people in the photo live?

2. What do you think the reaction of these people was when two white middle-aged women arrived in their village?

3. Why do you think these women went to the village?

VOCABULARY PREVIEW

A **Read the definitions of these key words and phrases that you will hear during the video.**

remote far away from cities and towns

dense forest area of land thick with trees

bonded formed a close relationship

mule train a line of mules (horselike animals) used to carry things, often on land with no roads

ambushed attacked suddenly by people who were hiding

taken aback surprised; shocked

escort to go somewhere with someone, often to protect them

fingers crossed a gesture that you make when you want to be lucky and have no harm come to you

warriors fighters

B Work with a partner and write vocabulary from A in the blanks in the sentences.

1. The Surma people live in a _____ area, so the two women needed a _____ to help carry their supplies.

2. The women _____ with the Surma. They attended wedding and births. So, they were _____ when they learned some Surma wanted to kill them.

3. Some Surma _____ were chosen to _____ the women out of the _____ so that they would be able to leave safely.

4. The women had their _____, hoping they would not be _____ and killed.

VIEWING

🖥 FIRST VIEWING

Watch the video, and then compare your first impressions with a partner. Talk about what you remember, what surprised you, and what interested you.

🖥 SECOND VIEWING

Watch the video again. Listen for the missing words and write them in the blanks.

1. And our _____ was to find the Surma people, who live in the southwest, close to the _____ of Sudan.

2. We understood that our mule train was going to be ambushed, and that we would not be allowed out _____.

3. And what had happened is, unknowingly, we had broken a cardinal _____ of their society.

4. We would have a big _____ honoring the chiefs of the Surma.

5. So at 3:00 a.m., we packed up in the dark, put a chief in _____ each mule all the way down the line, and headed out in the pitch black of the _____ with our breath held and our fingers crossed.

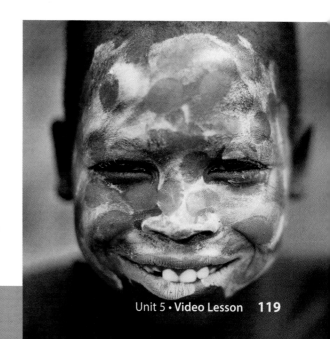

📺 THIRD VIEWING

Complete these notes as you watch the video. Write only important words, not full sentences, and abbreviate common words.

1. The journey in

2. Bonding w/the Surma

3. The problem

4. The feast

5. The journey out

ORAL SUMMARY

Use your notes to create an oral summary of the video with your partner. As you work together, add details to your notes that your partner included but you had missed.

DISCUSSION

Discuss the following questions with a classmate or in a small group.

1. What were some causes and some effects in the story told by Carol Beckwith?

2. What does Carol Beckwith mean when she says, "We're here to tell the tale"?

3. Give an example of a situation where you had a cultural misunderstanding. What caused the misunderstanding?

Videoscripts

Surviving an Avalanche

About two months ago, I got caught in a pretty serious avalanche. I went for 2,000 feet. Basically the whole mountainside came down.

When the avalanche happened, I had just finished filming with Jeremy Jones and Xavier de Le Rue in the Tetons. The temperatures were rising pretty significantly so there was a lot of change happening in the snow pack. We were aware of that; you know we've all spent a lot of time in the mountains, and we were trying to manage the terrain and the snow pack. And I was actually third on slope, and those two guys were up on the side on this little safe zone, and I just watched the whole mountain pretty much crack behind me, and I got caught in the avalanche.

I was, you know, probably a few hundred feet down. I was still on top, and I watched a bunch of these trees just snap in half in front of me and went over this big rollover, and I went to the bottom of the snow pack and just got crushed and held down for a while, and then I eventually resurfaced to the top.

You know, when you're at the bottom, you don't want it to stop because you know if it stops, they will never find you 'cause it was too big. So I came up to the top, and eventually you can feel the weight coming off of you. It's really kind of an unbearable amount of weight because it's like hundreds of tons of snow essentially.

And then I came back to the top and I kind of rolled over, and I was back on top of the snow pack. And I looked around me and for a moment, actually, I stopped being scared because just the magnitude of what I was caught in was so incredible that, you know, it was like I had the moment to pause and, you know, you don't generally feel that kind of power ever, especially in an uncontrolled environment.

I remember looking, too, and I looked down and I could see the entire avalanche path, and it was all— I knew I was going to the bottom of the valley and, you know, the trees are like that big and these are like 200, hundred-foot tall trees and I was like, okay, I'm going back to the bott— I'm going all the way and I went another thousand feet to the bottom. And I don't know what happened. I got to the bottom. I could feel it slowing down, and I popped right out at the toe of the avalanche.

You know, it took my partners 20 minutes—30 minutes to even get down, and they were 100 percent sure I was gone. I mean, they would have been less surprised if they had been talking to my ghost. When they showed up and they saw me, they were just— couldn't believe it.

Tristan da Cunha Oil Spill

Tristan da Cunha—it's the remotest island, remotest inhabited island on earth. And I was lucky enough to travel there this year. Unfortunately, I was also unlucky in that I arrived the same time that a ship wrecked on the island and spilled oil into the water.

And it was devastating. It was a big oil spill that affected a lot of Northern Rock Hopper Penguins, which are already endangered. And so I realized when I landed on this island and saw this, that there was no one else here. Nobody in the world knew about this. There was no communication; there was no way to transmit images.

This is an island that's completely disconnected. It's off the grid, and I happened to land there. So the first thing I did was take as many pictures of this as I could. I created a YouTube video. I published it immediately from the ship, and then I took more pictures and more video. And I Tweeted it. I put it out on Twitter, and it immediately got picked up by the blogosphere.

Now that word is a little outdated, but blogs are important because they're organic. And from this blog—you know we at *National Geographic*, we have an incredible news team—they took my footage, they took my pictures. They published it. They got it out there in the real press, and then this went to the *New York Times*.

But this kind of organic bubbling up of news, of being there, being in the middle of the ocean and capturing these things, this is something that all of you can do and all of you are doing it all the time. When I say, "Be there," I mean be wherever it is that you are. It could be in your own backyard. A lot of you live in Washington, D.C., where things are happening all the time, and believe it or not, you're part of this system where you are reporting.

People, Plants, and Pollinators

Dino Martins: Yes, I am an entomologist, and I know a lot of you think that's strange, but I hope I'll convince you by the end of the fifteen minutes I'm allotted that insects are actually the creatures that do run the world and that are truly, truly wonderful.

But something you may not know is that bees, honeybees, actually originate in East Africa. And just like humans migrated in waves out of Africa, so did honeybees. And the amazing thing with honeybees in Africa is there's a lot of diversity within Africa just like there's a lot of human diversity in Africa. And in East Africa, there are two fantastic varieties of honeybee that we get to work with, the lovely mountain honeybee, Monticola, which is a very gentle chocolate-colored species and produces lots and lots of honey. And then the Savannah or Dryland honeybee, Scutellata, which is not so gentle and not so calm, but also produces lots of honey.

And in addition to honeybees, another social bee that gets managed and that always surprises people to learn about are stingless bees. And Maria here is a beekeeper, a stingless beekeeper, on the slopes of Mount Meru in Tanzania. And you can see a view inside the stingless beehive there. And stingless bee honey—here are two different species of stingless bee honey, Iwele honey and Icore honey, which come from Western Kenya—is as valuable if not more valuable than honeybee honey, which all of these different communities produce.

So I told you a little bit about stingless bees because a lot of the work I'm trying to develop right now is managing and protecting stingless bees. And here is Stanley who is a stingless beekeeper in Western Kenya, at the Kakamega forest, and he keeps five different species of stingless bees. Those are the hives over there. And he even keeps species that scientists don't know about.

Now, bees pollinate crops and wild flowers, and a quick question to you. How many of you like coffee? Chocolate? Yeah. And those are just a couple of examples of two crops that would not exist without the actions of pollinators.

Woman: Today I've learned that there are so many types of bees. I only thought there was only one kind of bee. Today I have found out that there are several kinds of bees. It's so amazing. It's amazing.

Dino Martins: Thank you. And we've found at least 10 different types of bees just here in your shop.

And I have one request to leave you with. If you can spend just five minutes a day in the company of an insect, your life will never be the same again. Thank you.

Free Soloing with Alex Honnold

Jenkins: Free soloing has to be the ultimate in free climbing.

Honnold: It's always a beautiful day to go out soloing.

Jenkins: To free solo is to go without a rope, and to go without gear, to only have your rock shoes and your chalk bag and the power of the mind. It's also very profound. The reason it's probably the ultimate is because one wrong move, you fall, you die.

Honnold: Let me try that again.

Jenkins: And the person at the top of this game, and it's hard to even call this a game, is Alex Honnold. Alex Honnold is probably a perfect example— is someone who has not only trained very hard, but is unbelievably gifted. He is like Michael Jordan.

Honnold: I spend my whole year living in the van traveling from one destination to another. Yeah, I would say that Yosemite probably is the center of my climbing. That all my climbing goals, all training, all kind of revolves around things that I want to do in Yosemite. This is by far my favorite place for soloing because the walls are so inspiring. Like everything here is so big and that's what gets me excited about soloing stuff. One of the most memorable moments was pitch, like, 22 of The Nose. I put my rope away and I switched to just soloing. I just had a moment of, like, this is like surreally cool, I was, like, I can't believe I'm up here with no rope just climbing. Like, this is rad.

Jenkins: Now, Alex has now done the regular route on Half Dome free solo. So, for most people on this planet who are serious climbers, doing Half Dome in a day or two is considered fantastic. Alex did it in three hours, without a rope. He didn't work that route a hundred times, he just got up below it, looked up at it, and believed, absolutely believed, that it was well within his ability.

Honnold: And it seems like in this last season, I've sort of embraced the whole experience, you know, embraced the unpleasant parts, too. It's kind of cool to just look around, you know, enjoy the exposure, and be, like, this is why I'm here. This is awesome.

The Surma People

While we were working on our book, *African Ark*, over a five-year period in Ethiopia, we decided to go into a remote wilderness area in the southwest part of the country. And our goal was to find the Surma people, who live in the southwest, close to the border of Sudan.

There were no roads into the area. We were up and down over ten-thousand-foot mountains and through dense forests of Colobus monkeys, and we finally got to the Surma. And we spent five weeks with this very extraordinary group of people. We were the first white people in that particular area, so initially they were terrified at what had happened and how we had rubbed off our brown skin. And we made very, very close and dear friends. We accompanied them through births—to births, to marriages, to stick fights where they have some of the wildest fights on the continent in order to prove masculinity and win wives.

And at the end of this extraordinary five-week period, where we had really bonded with about 250 of the Surma, we prepared to leave. And the night before we were leaving, we understood that our mule train was going to be ambushed, and that we would not be allowed out alive. And we were extremely disarmed and taken aback by this because we felt we had made such extraordinary bonds with a small group of people in four villages.

And what had happened is, unknowingly, we had broken a cardinal rule of their society. They're an egalitarian people, and we had left out 13,000 other Surma people in establishing our close friendship with three villages. So they felt this was an unacceptable violation of their social system and that we shouldn't be allowed out of Surma land alive. So our guide, Zoga, decided to host a huge gathering of all the elders, and we would have a goat roast. We would have a big feast honoring the chiefs of the Surma.

And at the end of this wonderful day where the chiefs felt really delighted with what had happened, he asked them if they would be willing to escort us out of Surma land and if they'd be willing to get up at 3 a.m. in the morning, which they said, "Of course, we will; it would be our honor."

So at 3:00 a.m. we packed up in the dark, put a chief in between each mule all the way down the line, and headed out in the pitch black of the night with our breath held and our fingers crossed. And by sunrise, we looked up and we saw in the trees the Surma warriors with their Kalashnikovs and AK-47s, pointed at us. But when they saw their chiefs, none of them pulled the trigger. They all just sat there and allowed us to pass out until we got to the border, and we're here to tell the tale.

Images

Inside front cover: Jim Webb/National Geographic Stock, Andrew Evans/National Geographic Stock, Rebecca Hale/National Geogrpahic Creative, Jimmy Chin/National Geographic Stock, Carol Beckwith and Angela Fisher/photokunst, **1:** Laird S. Brown/National Geographic Stock, **2–3:** Leemage/Universal Images Group/Getty Images, **6:** Imagno/Hulton Archive/Getty Images, **7:** Nick Ledger/AWL Images/Getty Images, **8:** C Squared Studios/Photodisc/Getty Images, **9:** Vandeville Eric/ABACA/Newscom, **13:** James L. Stanfield/National Geographic Stock, **15:** Len Langevin/National Geographic Stock, **16:** Peter Macdiarmid/Staff/Getty Images Europe/Getty Images, **22–23:** Tim Laman/National Geographic Stock, **23:** ra photography/E+/Getty Images, **25:** Justin Guariglia/National Geographic Stock, **26–27:** Stela Tasheva/National Geographic My Shot/National Geographic Stock, **30–31:** Robin Smith/Stone Collection/Getty Images, **31:** Lovrencg/Fotolia, **32:** malahova/Fotolia, **32:** malahova/Fotolia, **32:** malahova/Fotolia, **32:** malahova/Fotolia, **32:** malahova/Fotolia, **32:** malahova/Fotolia, **33:** James P. Blair/National Geographic Stock, **37:** Jamie Grill/The Image Bank/Getty Images, **39:** Peter Cade/Iconica/Getty Images, **43:** Yoshikazu Tsuno/AFP/Image Collection, **44:** lightpoet/shutterstock, **44:** lightpoet/shutterstock, **44:** lightpoet/shutterstock, **44:** lightpoet/shutterstock, **44:** lightpoet/shutterstock, **45:** tuja66/fotolia, **45:** Ekaterina Bozhukova/Fotolia, **45:** Viktor/Fotolia, **45:** byggarn.se/Fotolia, **45:** Anson/Fotolia, **46–47:** Andrew Evans/National Geographic Stock, **47:** Kent Kobersteen/National Geographic Stock, **49:** Peter Carlsson/Getty Images, **50:** JIJI Press/Stringer/AFP/Getty Images, **51:** Dennis Macdonald/Photolibrary/Getty Images, **56–57:** Cristina De Paoli/National Geographic My Shot/National Geographic Stock, **60:** Andrew Rodriguez/Fotolia, **63:** Randy Olson/National Geographic Stock, **68:** Michael Melford/National Geographic Stock, **68:** George Grall/National Geographic Stock, **68:** George Grall/National Geographic Stock, **68:** Frans Lanting/National Geographic Stock, **68:** George Grall/National Geographic Stock, **69:** Ralph Lee Hopkins/National Geographic Stock, **69:** George Grall/National Geographic Stock, **69:** George Grall/National Geographic Stock, **69:** Barry Tessman/National Geographic Stock, **69:** Marc Moritsch/National Geographic Stock, **69:** George Grall/National Geographic Stock, **69:** Frans Lanting/National Geographic Stock, **69:** Roy Toft/National Geographic Stock, **70–71:** Amy Toensing/National Geographic Stock, **71:** George Grall/National Geographic Stock, **73:** David Allan Brandt/Iconica/Getty Images, **74–75:** Steve Winter/National Geographic Stock, **79:** Joel Sartore/National Geographic Stock, **79:** Joel Sartore/National Geographic Stock, **80:** picture5479/Fotolia, **81:** Bob Stefko/The Image Bank/Getty Images, **81:** Carl Mydans/Contributor/Time & Life Pictures/Getty Images, **86:** NBC Newswire via Getty Images, **86:** North Wind Picture Archives, **87:** Katherine Young/Hulton Archive/Getty Images, **87:** Maryann Groves/North Wind Picture Archives, **88–89:** Filippo Montefote/AFP/Getty Images, **93:** Archive Holdings Inc./Hulton Archive/Getty Images, **94–95:** Jimmy Chin/National Geographic Stock, **95:** Richard Nowitz/National Geographic Stock, **97:** Ralph Lee Hopkins/National Geographic Stock, **98–99:** Frans Lanting/National Geographic Stock, **104:** Valentin Casarsa/E+/Getty Images, **104:** Mike Powell/Allsport Concepts/Getty Images, **104:** Ross Woodhall/Cultura/Getty Images, **104:** Leland Bobbe/Photonica/Getty Images, **104:** Mitchell Funk/Photographer's Choice/Getty Images, **105:** North Wind Pictures Archives, **110:** Photo_Ma/Fotolia, **110:** Peter Cade/Iconica/Getty Images, **111:** Fuse/Getty Images, **111:** Matthias Tunger/Photographer's Choice RF/Getty Images, **111:** Jochen Tack/arabianEye/Getty Images, **111:** John Lund/Photodisc/Getty Images, **112–113:** Joel Sartore/National Geographic Stock, **117:** Peter Essick/National Geographic Stock, **118–119:** Carol Beckwith and Angela Fisher/photokunst, **119:** Gamma-Rapho via Getty Images